THE IDEA OF A CATHOLIC COLLEGE

THE IDEA OF
A CATHOLIC COLLEGE

BY JOHN JULIAN RYAN

SHEED & WARD · NEW YORK · 1945

Copyright, 1945, Sheed & Ward, Inc.

Manufactured in the United States of America

Designed by Stefan Salter

TO MARY THE MOTHER OF GOD
SEAT OF WISDOM
VIRGIN MOST PRUDENT

CONTENTS

FOREWORD

Not every one will agree with all of the points made by Professor Ryan in his challenging book on THE IDEA OF A CATHOLIC COLLEGE. Some will complain that certain of his proposals look too far forward; others will suspect that a few of his ideas look back with nostalgia to a Catholic culture now long-past, a culture which may never return and which, in its ancient forms, at least, need not return so far as the essential ends of the Church and of its teaching mission are concerned.

It is, however, precisely the merit of Professor Ryan's book that, whatever personal theories he may weave into his argument, he is constantly faithful to the essential ends of the Church's educative work. He gives fresh statement to old problems which have a way of recurring and which will certainly recur to vex educators in the post-war college world. He re-states the question for innumerable debates which cannot be other than helpful to those who must devise curricula and programs for our colleges henceforth. Even more interesting, he traces a philosophy of education which, properly meditated, should clear the air of the heaviness that inevitably settles around all pedagogical discussions.

Saint Paul once set forth the ultimate purpose of all Catholic education when he spoke of the manner in which the image of Christ must be "built up" in every soul. Professor Ryan has attempted to provide a tentative blueprint for builders of that image in our college students.

It is an original sketch, yet faithful to the basic elements of our tradition. It does not forget that the image of Christ is primarily spiritual and supernatural. But neither does it forget that the integral image of the Incarnate Son of God must include reflections of Christ the Human, the Healer, the Poet and the Craftsman.

Professor Ryan's contentions may not settle all the problems of the Catholic college course. They will, however, stimulate some arguments, and out of these may come the solutions of countless collegiate difficulties. On technical details, the solutions may not always be those of Professor Ryan. The general spirit of them and their informing purpose must, nonetheless, necessarily be that which he sets for the Catholic college when he writes: "All the arts and sciences [taught in it] will conduce to one all-encompassing end, that of enabling [the student] to live abundantly through obeying the highest law of man's nature as explained by our Lord, the law of Love."

RICHARD J. CUSHING
Archbishop of Boston

THE IDEA OF A CATHOLIC COLLEGE

INTRODUCTION

THIS BOOK is not a treatise, an invective, or a plea. It is not primarily concerned with exploring a subject, excoriating opponents, defending a set of principles, or calling attention to a "crying need." These things, if it does them at all, it does quite incidentally and by implication only. Nor is it the kind of book that blazes a philosophic trail up to a clearing and then leaves the reader there, with the suggestion that he build a city at that point by merely following out the principles learned thus far. It is something a little more instructive than that: it is a design; a blue-print.

And because it is a blue-print of a normal, rather than of an exceptional, institution, it is intended to be used either as a plan or as a yard-stick: as a plan by anyone interested in founding a wholly Catholic college; as a yard-stick by anyone already managing a Catholic college or trying to frame a proper concept of one. For professional and non-professional readers alike, the book should act as a crystallizing agent, enabling them to define their ideas sharply by setting before them something definite, which they can either accept or reject.

Since it has this purpose, the book is to be read critically. The author hopes that the reader will submit it to the most acid questions, specific as well as general; questions such as: "Is this really the most Catholic answer possible? Is the end here ascribed to Catholic education by the author its true end? Is this the end that provides us with the principle whereby we are to integrate that education? Is it true that the Catholic college must be designed to train its students for the way of life set forth here as the most Catholic? Does the author show a proper appreciation of the kinds of students such a college should and would deal with? Hence, does he see what kinds of teaching and what kind of curriculum are required for training students to live truly Catholic lives in a spirit profoundly Catholic?" In short, the author expects that the reader will examine every answer given here searchingly, testing it always with the decisive question: "Is there any other answer as essentially Catholic as, or better than, this?"

But if the book is to be read thus critically, it gains thereby the right to be read fairly: the reader is asked to reserve judgment on the plan here proposed until he has grasped it as a whole. For, reading the book straight through, he will almost certainly find that many of his objections have been met in the course of it, or at least, that many of them have been considered and dealt with in the final chapter called "Objections." Otherwise, he would do well to turn to that chapter as soon as he feels an objection coming on.

This book was written, in other words, to gain not mere agreement from the captious, but clear-eyed consent from the enterprising. It is intended to be, not a day-dream of an educational Utopia, but a blue-print of a truly Catholic college—a definite, practical plan which the author would like to carry out or aid others in carrying out. It sets forth as concretely as possible the ends, the methods, the materials, and the instruments which would be sanctioned by saint, sage, teacher, parent, and student alike. It is intended to be the design of the kind of Catholic college which both ought to be and can be. May it also prove to be the design of one that soon will be.

2

CHAPTER ONE

AIMS

Since this book is intended to be a blue-print of the Catholic college, for use either as a norm or as a basic plan, it will lay out, first of all, the ends which this institution should attain, and then attempt to describe the means it may best use for attaining these ends. The book will deal, therefore, mainly with the following questions:

First, what is the aim of Catholic life; that is, of the kind of life for which the Catholic college should train its students?

Second, what, as a consequence, must be the aims of the Catholic college; and how will these give it its integrating principle and determine its essential pattern?

Third, who are its students, and what are the educational problems which they raise?

Fourth, what kind of curriculum will be needed if these students are to be trained for these ends?

Fifth, what kinds of teachers and teaching methods will be required here?

The book will end with a few suggestions on incidental matters and with a treatment of certain probable objections to its proposals.

Now, before we seek to determine what a normal Catholic life is, we may well pause for a moment and consider carefully what the word *normal* refers to— exactly what a norm is and is not. It is not to be confused with an average, on the one hand, nor with the impossibly ideal, on the other. It is simply the pattern of that which both ought to be and can be, by which we are guided in perfecting what is. It is therefore the kind of standard which doctors, for example, work by as a matter of course. No doctor ever expects to see a perfectly normal man; but, for all that, he always keeps in mind the possibility of such a person, in order to help his patients approximate him. A doctor does not say, "The average man is in an average state of health; therefore I shall be content if I bring my sub-average man, my patient, to this state." Nor does he say, "I shall not be content unless I can get my patient to grow a new leg in place of the old one I had to amputate; or a new appendix for the one I was forced to remove." He guides himself by the ideal of perfect normality; but he is satisfied with the closest approach to it possible under the circumstances. So here. The Catholic way of life (and the Catholic method of education) about to be described is normal in the sense that it is something at which to aim: it is not a picture of what the average Catholic is all too often content with; nor of what only a St. Francis or a St. John of the Cross could attain; it is a picture of what we should all try to attain as well as we can—of what St. Francis might do if he had to run a shop in Suburbia.

The easiest way, perhaps, for us to visualize clearly the norm of a Catholic life is to begin with some clear-cut marking out of what the Catholic *cannot* do: what ends he cannot follow, what methods he cannot employ.

Well, then, first of all, he cannot live a life that is, in any sense, tepidly religious. He cannot delude himself into supposing that he is "a good Catholic" when he divides his life into two parts, the religious and the secular, and then goes on to live the one unintelligently and the other intelligently: a moron in church, a "live wire" in the office. A true Catholic, in other words, cannot regard his religion either as something apart or as something secondary, less important than his business or social affairs and affecting them only indirectly.

He is not, then, *normally* Catholic when he cherishes as adequate such meager notions of Catholicism as: That the Church is merely something for keeping us straight, an instrument between us and God which we shall wisely make use of if we want to be assured of ultimate happiness while not sacrificing any real happiness here on earth. That the Church is a sound moral adviser—although it should confine itself to matters strictly religious. That it is a source of consolation and a means of getting favors from God through His saints. That the Mass, the sacraments, contemplation, corporal works of mercy, the study of the Faith, and the like, are all the work of priests and religious. That a congregation is a mere group of individuals who, because they happen to belong to the same parish, go to the same church on Sundays and Holy Days. That Latin and the liturgy, like theology, are beyond him; hence they had better be left to priests and scholarly enthusiasts. That, in short, religion is just one "element," not the principal determinant, of life.

Nor is it normal for the Catholic to conduct his secular activities on the basis of suppositions like the following: That it is all right for him to spend his days and nights in getting as much as possible and giving as little as possible; in putting others out of business by "legitimate" competition; in nervously watching the fluctuations of the

5

stock market; in supplying luxuries for the rich or the foolishly extravagant while ignoring the needs of slum-dwellers; in bribing others (or in allowing himself to be bribed) to go through motions before an assembly line or a press, with neither skill nor charity, simply to gain the luxuries and the pay of "a high standard of living"; in withholding necessary patents or concealing trade secrets; in eliminating competitors through deadly price-cutting, high-pressure salesmanship, pandering to the corrupted tastes of customers, adulteration, the insinuation of substitutes.

The really good Catholic (as opposed to the kind who is all too frequently called so) could never be content with treating workers as if they should be satisfied with the comforts and care granted to a race-horse; with never dedicating his work to God; with spending little or no time and effort in training for and practising the arts required for properly participating in the Mass, receiving the sacraments, making use of the sacramentals, praying, contemplating, performing works of mercy, restoring the social order in Christ. It is certainly not upon the life of a "success" that a good Catholic can look with any equanimity—even when the family of such a success does seem to be well taken care of: well-housed, well-clothed, well-fed, and expensively educated.

No; the Catholic has no right to the kind of life here depicted, with its terrible cleavage of the spiritual from the bodily, the religious from the secular, Heaven from earth. For he must know that, as St. Paul says (St. Paul who always meant just what he said), nothing, *absolutely nothing,* not one single thing we do is of any real value unless it is done in charity. Herein is to be found the

6

first necessity and the highest good of our every act and of our every institution: that which is at once the *sine qua non* and the *summum bonum*. For, as he says: "I may speak with every tongue that men and angels use; yet, if I lack charity, I am no better than echoing bronze, or the clash of cymbals. I may have powers of prophecy, no secret hidden from me, no knowledge too deep for me; I may have utter faith, so that I can move mountains; yet if I lack charity, I count for nothing. I may give away all that I have, to feed the poor; I may give myself up to be burnt at the stake; if I lack charity, it goes for nothing."

Specifically, then, this means that *the Catholic must so live that he shall, by his every thought, word, and deed, in all the actions of his mind, heart, and soul, come closer and closer to God, working towards intimate union with Him, not only in the next world, in the Beatific Vision, but also in this world, through incorporation with Christ in the Mystical Body.* As a member of this Mystical Body, the Catholic will be given the grace and the means for becoming one with God in three main ways: through knowledge, becoming one with Him by intellectual assimilation, oneness of mind; through purely spiritual assimilation, becoming one with Him by participation in His life, by means of the Mass, the Eucharist, the other sacraments—receiving His life, His presence, and His grace so as to be animated and nourished thereby; and through conformity of will and heart: becoming one with Him by doing, in Charity, what He would have us do; loving as He wants us to love; using our talents to the fullest in serving others for His sake and in restoring all things in Him.

Simply as an individual, therefore, the Catholic may well try to live up to the prayer of St. Francis:

Lord, make me an instrument of Thy peace!
Where there is hatred, let me sow love;
Where there is injury, pardon;
Where there is doubt, faith;
Where there is despair, hope;
Where there is darkness, light;
Where there is sadness, joy.

O Divine Master, grant that I may
Not so much seek
To be consoled as to console;
To be understood as to understand;
To be loved as to love!
For it is in giving that we receive;
It is in pardoning that we are pardoned;
It is in dying that we are born to eternal life.

But the Catholic knows that even as an individual he is best able to live up to this prayer by making himself a fit and living member of the Mystical Body of Christ; prosecuting daily, to the best of his ability, all the arts necessary for understanding Its significance and nature; for being inspired by Its love; for assimilating Its graces; for becoming one with It in all Its life. These, his purely spiritual activities, will be both central and dominant in his life.

His secular life, however, must also be religious in tone and motive. He will strive to make his work itself a form of meditation, prayer, contemplation, and Charity. He will be animated by a love of perfection which is in part an effect, in part a cause, of his love of the Ultimate Perfection, God. His human art will lead him to some appreciation of the Divine Art manifested in the Incarnation. In laboring, he will be praying; in following the vocation for which, by his talents, he is destined, he will be doing God's will humbly and unselfishly, performing a high and steady act of Charity. He will, in brief, try to make his life an *integrally* spiritual one: a life in which he passes at need, not from unspiritual to spiritual activities, but from religious secular actions to religious spiritual—as his vocation requires.

Naturally, he will try to produce the best of which he is capable: things or performances that are lofty in intention and superb in technique. His interest will be in filling needs, not in making money or expressing himself; and he will take care of the neediest first. He will never aim directly at the making of profit, but only at getting, with reasonable certainty, enough to live on. The things which he makes will be good, rather than merely salable: he will not pander, "giving the public what it wants" or pretending that the inexpert customer knows better than he, the expert craftsman. He will charge a fair price to all, but give freely of his products, as well as of his services, to the poor. In carrying on his craft, he will choose, not the material most profitable to him, but that which, for his given purpose, is best; not the easiest, least costly, not a fame-getting technique, but the most effective. The symbolic as well as the purely utilitarian values of a product will be of concern to him; and his designs he will not make eye-catching or fashionable, but splendidly right. To put it succinctly, he will try, in Charity, to make the most needed things as well as they can be made, and to get them into the hands of those who need them.

He will also strive to make his relations with fellow craftsmen as charitable as those with his patrons. His effort here will be to establish or maintain a system directed towards producing value at a fair and fixed price: one in which every master craftsman sets high standards of work; maintains just and fixed fees; cooperates to eliminate unfair practices; disciplines severely any commercial members of the craft; takes in apprentices no matter how poor (or how well-to-do) they are; gives these a fair, just, and professionally thorough apprenticeship, looking out for their spiritual welfare first and treating them as adopted sons. Negatively, he would work to ban all "salesmanship," all so-called "free" enterprise in which the strong are free to eliminate the weak; all monopoly and similar swinishness.

The members of his craft would swear to a common code, support one another in sickness and death, share their knowledge of technical advances, cooperate with other craft groups, and, in general, live and work together in the communal Charity of the Mystical Body.

They would, therefore, respect one another as fully responsible human beings—cooperating not as employers and employees, as owners and hands, but as masters and apprentices. In the system for which the Catholic should strive, no man should be able to command another to do anything he either would not or could not do himself. No master craftsman would be allowed to divide the work by time-and-motion units: apprentices could not be de-humanized by mere repetitive mechanical action requiring no use of will and intelligence. Large units of either product or service would be divided into their whole natural parts; and each part would be assigned to one group of apprentices and masters, each apprentice being trained, as is every interne, in all the necessary techniques, from those of designing to those of assembling. Each worker would thus be assured of the joy of acting meritoriously and creatively, in charitable and enthusiastic co-operation with his fellow craftsmen.

Here, then, we have a fairly clear sketch of the general way of life to be desired by every Catholic, the way for which he should be trained. The next question is, what is the likelihood that it can ever be assured: must the Catholic college, therefore, aim at something less ideal?

The calm answer, rendered after a study of both the past and the present, would seem to be, that this way of life is possible because it has been and is being followed, almost to the very letter.

For what has been outlined here resembles very closely indeed the life of the ordinary country doctor in America today. Consider the ideals and methods of this man. He sets out primarily to serve his fellow-men, binding himself in honor to risk his life if necessary for their sakes. He does *not* set out to make a fortune. He charges a fair price for fair value, giving his services gratis to the poor and needy. To make sure that this fair value is always given, he sets high standards of both knowledge and experience—either alone being insufficient—as prerequisites to the practicing of medicine. So far from trying to "eliminate" his fellow doctors from competition with him —through advertising, price-cutting, the monopolizing of trade secrets (patent medicines), mass production methods, or financial chicanery—he does just the opposite:

he goes out of his way never to speak a derogatory word of another, never to advertise, never to split fees, never to patent a medicine or an instrument (instead, he passes on all news of his discoveries), never to haggle or to fight for his "ten percent discount for cash within thirty days", never to put a patient into bankruptcy, and so on. He does all that he can to see that both the public and the medical profession are treated as justly and charitably as possible; that men who wish to lead a dedicated unselfish life in the service of mankind may do so without interference from money-grubbers inspired by "enlightened self-interest" and aided by fellow professionals like themselves.

Naturally, most doctors do not live at the level on which the Catholic should live: they act out of "a common regard for humanity"; and not, ordinarily, inspired by man's highest motive, truly Christian Charity. But here again, Nature at its best so closely parallels Grace, that the ways of the one can easily be completed and transformed by the other. If men taking oaths by Aesculapius and Hippocrates can arrive, in a highly materialistic society, at a system such as that of the American Medical Association, how well should those men be able to perfect it who do not merely take oath by, but fervently live in, Christ the Healer.

"All well and good," comes the objection. "What you say here is all right for doctors and for professional men in general. But it does not apply to ordinary occupations. Surely, it cannot be contended that anything like the way of life you picture can be followed by everyone."

Yes; it can.

The way of life here described is not for the few only;

it is the norm for *every* vocation, no matter how lowly. *For every way of life not only should be, but can be, made professional: all men can follow, with professional skill, some richly charitable vocation.*

They can do so because every form of work, from the composing of a liturgical chant to the digging of a ditch, can be executed in a purely professional spirit, with a purely professional code, by a purely professional method, after purely professional training. It is, in fact, both unsound and uncharitable to consider even the lowest forms of manual labor as essentially different from that of the physician: the difference between the forms of work is one of degree, not of kind.

For if we look closely at the work of the doctor and then (to choose the most crucial instance possible) at that of the ditch-digger, we shall see that although they do differ as carried on at present, they need not differ, nor ought they to differ. Viewed properly, as Our Lord would view them, they turn out to be essentially alike: they require the same mental and moral dispositions; they exercise the same faculties; they even follow the same universal principles of technique.

It is certainly almost self-evident that the love for God and neighbor, Charity, is not a grace peculiarly reserved to medical men. If the eminent surgeon can follow heroically his vocation for this motive, so can the ditch-digger, inspired by exactly the same Charity. The ditch-digger too can rejoice—give him but the chance—in using his work as a means for achieving the leisure for contemplation and spiritual exercises. Hard as it seems at first to believe, he too can see the Perfection of God as it shines through the perfection of a well-dug trench. He too can hold himself to the giving of full value for a fair and reasonable price. He too can acquire the skill worthy of the name of art. This fact becomes obvious when we pause to consider, first, that it is no easy thing to dig a ditch properly; and second (as has been pointed out before) that if a philanthropist were to offer, say, $25,000 a year for the best dug trench of perhaps six by four by twelve, to be completed within a carefully defined time, it would not be long before men who were originally scoffers would discover how much of an art ditch-digging could be. They would see, in fact, that it was quite as great an art as one they now prize highly, golf; that, properly, it should have one set of spades for breaking ground, another for digging at medium depth, another for full depth, and so on, to say nothing of the analyses of stance, trajectory, types of dirt, types of obstacle, position of digger in relation to cart, and the rest.

Nor is there any reason why masters of the art of digging should not hold themselves to a code; form an association of excavators;* afford strict training, moral as well as mental, for their apprentices; and regulate themselves for the good of the public as well as for their own good: be, in short, a sound professional association.

To smile at the mere possibility of this is, it would seem, to betray either a vast ignorance of the medieval guild system, or an un-Christian, white-collar snobbishness resulting from a misprizing of manual skill in favor of nice, clean paper work. As for this absurd prejudice that work cannot be morally or technically beautiful if it

---

* For their work would naturally consist of all forms of excavation, complex as well as simple, from that for big buildings, tunnels, and wells up to that for great dams.

is expended on material that is unlovely, one may well ask: what, on that score, is the difference between digging a trench in war and digging an even cleaner one in peace? Or who would venture to say that the entrails which the eminent surgeon must finger are, to the eyes alone, any more dignified and glamorous than the entrails of the earth?

If the views presented thus far are sound, it is clear that the Catholic student is to be trained in *all* the arts that must be prosecuted simultaneously in leading a wholly Christian life: not only those required for saving his soul, but also those required for living, and making a living, in a civilized society.

Thus he is to be shown how to lead a life in which, through incorporation in the Mystical Body of Christ, he is made ready for sharing in the Beatific Vision in the next world and for sharing in the Life of that Body (the continuing Christ-Life) in this, and for aiding others to share in It. And it therefore becomes evident that a Catholic college, to be worthy of its name, must train its students how best, in Charity, to participate in the Mass, to receive the sacraments, to make use of the sacramentals, to pray (liturgically as well as privately), to contemplate, appreciate, study, and work. Developing the natural faculties of its students to their utmost—their imaginations, intellects, and wills—it should promote all those sound habits of craftsmanship and industry, of economic, political, and social cooperation, of scientific investigation, of discrimination, and of philosophic and theological contemplation that will aid them, as members of the Mystical Body of Christ, to regain the integrity lost at the Fall, to sanctify themselves, to sacramentalize * the world and society, while making a living (whether as professional men, business men, or craftsmen) and to share at all times as intimately as possible in the work of the Trinity, now and forever.

* Sacramentalize: The word is here used in its broadest sense; that is, to mean, "through Grace, of which the Church is the treasury, to put Nature to the service of Grace."

CHAPTER TWO

THE STUDENT

THE ENDS OF THE Catholic college having been determined, the next questions which would seem to arise naturally are those concerning the means to be used in attaining these ends: namely, what kind of curriculum should we favor; what should the integrating principles of that curriculum be; and what teaching methods should be followed? But before we can hazard any suggestions on these points, it is necessary that we should pause and determine exactly what kind of student it is who is to be trained for the Catholic way of life. Like the football coach at the beginning of a season, we must consider with care the question, What is the nature of our "material": what is the nature of the young American? in fact, what is the nature of man himself?

For the teacher, much more than this or that other artist, cannot afford to labor under delusions about the material with which he is dealing. A teacher can no more succeed in training a young man by treating him as "the most highly endowed of the anthropoids" than a horseman can succeed in training a Kentucky thoroughbred by treating him as if he were an exceptionally good jackass. A sound craftsman has to know and respect his material: he must know to his finger-tips its advantages and disadvantages; he must be deeply versed in its tendencies and habits—what it likes to do; what it does not like to do; and how great is the spread between what he wants it to do and what it likes to do. The fundamental questions that arise here, then, are these: What is there in man, especially in a modern young American, that makes him amenable to the training we have in mind? What is there in him that does not? What is the spread between what we should like to have him become and what he is to start with?

From our analysis of Catholic life, it is clear what kind of person we should like the student to become. Could he exist at all, the perfect product of the perfect Catholic college would be, first of all, a saint; second, a craftsman or artist (that is, of course, a conscientious man of skill, no matter what his work—a professionally minded man who is an "artist in his own field," whether that field be law, education, medicine, business, politics, science, or the fine arts). As a man of Charity, he would have the most intense love for God and neighbor, being animated by it in all his actions at all times. As a man of Prudence, he would see "instinctively" how to follow God's will in all things. As a man of Wisdom, he would see God as the first Reality of all things, whether in nature or in destiny. As a man of Art, he would know how to make things well (whether objects or performances), in accordance with the principles of common-sense, of experience, of science, of philosophy, and of the insights of talent. Through steady training, he would be, in the best sense, a man of habit; it would be second-nature for him to exercise the technical virtues: he would be free of timidity and tension, working aptly and gracefully; he would be courageous enough to face honestly and solve afresh the peculiar problems of each new task, neither despising nor over-prizing the methods of the past; he would be industrious enough to lavish care upon his work; humble enough never to regard it simply as a means of self-expression; self-controlled; perfection-loving; temperate. In short, he would be a person properly motivated, properly taught, and properly trained, to do the right (the Christian) thing in the right (the Christian) way.

Now, because of the student's nature and elementary training it is both easy and difficult to aid him to approximate this norm, this pattern of qualities. For man is, of course, neither divine nor bestial; he is neither an animal nor a god, but an animal in the image and likeness of God, a creature who, as we see if we look about us, is forever impelled to seek God, even when he cannot recognize Him. As Godlike, he must seek God (for like loves like); as creature he is in danger of fainting before he finds his Goal. He turns towards the Splendor of the Good and the True much as a plant turns, blindly but surely, towards the sunlight: man is spiritually photo-tropic; his soul seeks the light; and the Light it seeks is the radiance of God. So anxious is he to find it quickly and near at hand that in his creatureliness he basks in the artificial sunlight of his own false gods: Comfort; Efficiency; the State; Medical Progress; Science. For all his blindness, he shows, especially when he is young, that there is something in him that drives him unceasingly, something to awaken fully, direct, and channel.

Being in the image and likeness of God, in fact, he is properly to be viewed as a *bonum diffusivum sui*—as a good that seeks to spread itself. Just as a good doctor could never think of keeping to himself his discoveries or his services, so (and supremely) "out of the goodness of His Heart," neither could God. Or, to put this in proper order, because God, by His very Nature, overflowed with Goodness (to such an extent, indeed, that He made things that they might share in this Goodness), so when He created His highest creature in His own image and likeness, He gave to that creature, *as his highest joy,* the Godlike possibility of receiving and spreading, especially to those in need, whatever of Good lay under his dominion—the privilege, that is, of cooperating in the diffusion of God's Goodness.

Now, a young man, feeling intensely his immaturity, longs deeply for both completion and intense experience. If, then, his training makes him certain that these yearnings are to be answered by seeking God and by acting, as far as possible, as God would act—with utmost generosity, he will obviously go far. The forces which a good teacher can tap, then, are both near the surface and immeasurably deep: were the student not a creature of dis-integrity, they would almost of themselves assure his salvation.

But because of the effects of Original and Actual Sin, he is a creature of dis-integrity. His powers are weakened through being at odds one with another: swayed by concupiscence or wrath, his intellect is imprudent, his will malicious. His unsteady mind can arrive at truth only by painful efforts at concentration. His gaze does not pierce deeply: he plumbs the truth only by experiment and painful reasoning. A doubting Thomas, he attains understanding, conviction, and appreciation of the most vital truths only by putting his hands into his own, as well as Christ's, wounds. It is idle for him to memorize something of which he has had no experience—as idle as for him to try to analyze the soul of a nation that he has never seen. One of his greatest difficulties is that his sense and his reasoning, his imagination and his intellect, do not work interpenetratively: he can know a general truth but fail to see that it applies or is manifested in this or that case; or he can appreciate somewhat this or that particular problem without seeing that it implies or destroys a whole working-theory.

Practically, he finds that he has to deal with himself as if he were not only a stupid, but a wilful child: that he has to learn by making a fool of himself and then analyzing his error humbly and trying again; that there is a great deal of difference between knowing how a thing is done and knowing how to do it; that it requires energy, skill, self-control, and much practice to make his nervous system and his mind into good instruments; that, if he is to succeed at all, he must learn, with each new art, how to overcome his two great enemies, timidity and tension.

Above all, because he feels himself to be a mysterious creature who is something more than a creature, he has a deep sense both of inadequacy and of worth. He knows himself to be stupid, perverse, guilty; yet at the same time, he is bewildered by the realization that he is, after all, a creature somehow sacred, an inviolable person. As a result, he may easily develop what is commonly, and improperly, called an inferiority complex—properly, an inferiority feeling. Because he cannot be absolutely certain just how he will act until he finds himself in the thick of the action (what speaker, for example, is ever perfectly sure how well he will speak on a given occasion?) and because he cannot see himself as others see him or come to an exact estimate of his stupidity, perversity, or sinfulness, he tries desperately to attain a well founded self-assurance, or, at the very least, to avoid self-contempt. So it is that if he sees others laugh when he "sticks his neck out," he will give up making even reasonable attempts at improvement, taking ordinary risks; or he may limit himself to doing only that which he knows he can do well. If teachers sarcastically set about "taking him down a peg," he may either give up or try to outwit them, demonstrating to himself, in one or other way, that he does amount to something: showing off, attracting attention or pity, excusing himself, dissipating—all to prove to himself that he is not the failure that he appears; that he has never failed to get whatever affection and respect he deserved, or at least its equivalent. What he is greatly in need of, then, is proper appreciation, an appreciation at once just and loving: an affection which is clear-headed but encouraging, charitable but enlightening; one which keeps him always aware of how much God and good men love him when he does the best he can in un-self-regarding Charity and humble enough to enjoy both his mistakes and his triumphs in an honest appreciation of facts.

The American boy or young man in particular has in many ways been rendered difficult to educate. He has usually been given a wrong view of himself and of the purpose of his life, the view of a pious and scholarly Philistine; and has been so well trained in accordance with this view that he considers any other "unnatural" or "too idealistic." He is likely to feel that Success is important and that, as a consequence, so too are marks. He has been told that knowledge is power (even though the Devil can quote Scripture), and that it is an end in itself (even though there is only one such, namely, God). The system of education in which he has been trained has indirectly convinced him that the suppositions on which it is based must be true, namely: that men are by nature selfish; that it is more "natural" that they should compete than that they should cooperate; that self-respect is a proper motive for a Christian; that formulae and words are more important than thoughts, and thoughts are more important than realities; that it is better to know many things than to be master of a few skills—it being vitally necessary "to cover the ground"; that one should learn facts and absorb methods, instead of learning methods and absorbing facts; that virtue has little or nothing to do with skill.

Now, if all this—the good and the bad alike—is true of the kind of student now entering our American colleges, it is perhaps even more true of the kind of student who should be entering them—the kind of boy for whom the Catholic college as such should be designed in these times. For that student, ideally, should be neither older than sixteen nor younger than fifteen. This, for economic reasons, for pedagogical reasons, and for spiritual reasons, which have been pointed out by various eminent educators for some time now. Economically, students need to be through with their college training early if they are to finish their university or professional school training and be in a position to get married before they are grey-beards. Pedagogically, the fact is that the last two years of high school have too frequently become sorry and pointless imitations of the first year or so of college; hence they may be a waste of time.* Spiritually, students of fifteen

* For the sake of those who are fearful of radical changes, it may be well to point out that the adoption of the policies here advocated will not result in the disruption of the high schools. It will not turn them into two-year institutions, nor will it throw the teachers of their Junior and Senior classes out of work. The high schools could continue to give four-year courses for those students who could not go to college, merely transforming their present Junior and Senior courses into the Freshman and Sophomore college courses suggested in this

or sixteen are in an excellent condition for college training: this is the age of the unspoiled mind, of intense enthusiasm, and of high resolve. Not to capture the untarnished, heroic spirit of early youth and train it for the highest ends, for which it is searching, is both stupid and tragic.

What the teacher in the Catholic college may expect to deal with, then, is a young man capable of profound spiritual enthusiasms, good-hearted, loyal, fundamentally sound, who is nevertheless not too well versed in either the primary crafts or the religious arts; moderately disciplined; commercialistic; a little soft; fearful of making a fool of himself; uninspired. Such is our material.

---

book. Part of the high school teachers would then stay on; part of them would become teachers of the college Freshman and Sophomore courses, with the college teachers moving up to higher grades, professional schools, and institutes.

CHAPTER THREE

THE CURRICULUM

HAVING NOW determined the aims of the Catholic college and the nature of its students, we can next consider the curriculum which might best be suited to the accomplishment of these aims. Such a curriculum would obviously need to comprise the arts which might be called beatific, those required for attaining earthly happiness through sacramentalization and, concurrently, heavenly happiness through incorporation with Christ and apprenticeship under Him as Master. Hence, the two main courses in the outline of studies here proposed are: practical theology (ascetics); and practical philosophy (technics). All other subjects are to be regarded as purely tributary to one or other of these main courses.

This curriculum, it should be observed, is remedial as well as perfective: neither one nor the other alone, but both. Its courses have been chosen and designed, in part at least, to aid the student to regain the integrity lost at the Fall, through training the intellect not to be imprudent, the will not to be malicious, the concupiscible not to be concupiscent, the irascible not to be infirm—restoring him, as far as possible, to his natural life and preparing him for his supernatural. The courses have also been chosen, of course, with all the positive supernatural ends in view that were discussed in the first chapter of this book, as well as with the purpose of enabling the student to integrate himself transcendentally: to make his actions and his life as a whole good, true, *and* beautiful, not merely good or true or beautiful.

The principal course, practical theology, is primarily a course of training. It is, first, a form of spiritual inspiration and coaching—a kind of not too strenuous year-long retreat; second, a training in the appreciation of the depth and beauty of Wisdom; third, a course in speculative theology; and fourth, quite incidentally, a course in apologetics. It presupposes that the acquisition of knowledge would be made subsidiary to the student's advancement in charity and skill; knowledge here is not to be cherished for its own sake, or for the overcoming of heretics.*

One other thing, perhaps, is to be noted: this curriculum has been designed with the notion that the student should be given all the essentials of his whole course of study as early as possible. He is to be shown at the very outset, certainly by the end of the first year, how to do all those things *somehow* which at the end of his training he will be doing well: that is, how to contemplate, philosophize, meditate, perform works of mercy, worship privately and liturgically, appreciate, study, and work. The last three years of his training are to be given over to refining, deepening, clarifying his knowledge of the principles he has learned in the first year, and primarily to making it a matter of second nature for him to obey them skilfully.

* It should perhaps be recalled here that even Truth, although it is usually best sought *as if* it were an end in itself, is ultimately not so: God alone being that end. As St. Paul, St. Thomas, and St. Bonaventure affirm, knowledge of a truth, even the most profound, will distract from God (the Truth) when it is really prized for itself alone.

The curriculum would run as follows:

FRESHMAN YEAR

Religion: General Survey in Liturgical Order
Logic: Written and Spoken Controversy and Explanation
Ecclesiastical Latin and Choral Singing
Philosophy: General Survey (Technics)
The Art of Studying: Brief Course in Scheduling, Note-
    taking, Memorizing, and so forth
Physical Training
Literature: Aesthetic and Moral Appreciation through
    Composition and Analysis
Mathematics: Fundamental Concepts
Crafts: Gardening; Carpentry; Lettering

SOPHOMORE YEAR

Religion: Christ
Greek: New Testament in the Original
Natural Science: Fundamentals of Science and Cosmology
Psychology: Man (The Three Main Views of Him)
Literature: Advanced Writing and Analysis (a Continua-
    tion of the Freshman Course)

JUNIOR YEAR

Religion: The Mystical Body
Philosophy: The Appreciation of Beauty
Economics: The Guildsman's View
The Old Testament
Christian Courtesy: Applied Ethics
Biology

SENIOR YEAR

Religion: Survey in Terms of the Mass, the Sacraments, and Prayer

Politics: *The Republic*; *The City of God*; *The Federalist Papers*

Philosophy: Ontology and Natural Theology

History: The Papacy and Liberalism

Physiology

Throughout all four years: Mathematics, Choral Singing, Crafts, and Physical Training

The following brief descriptions will give some notion of what these courses cover. The reader should be warned, perhaps, that although these descriptions are fairly full, they must not be considered complete; nor should any one of the courses be regarded as independent of the others and judged in isolation from them. For all the subjects in a curriculum should, in a sense, inter-penetrate: they are to be evaluated in the light of their ultimate and integrating purposes and of their mutual helpfulness, their coalescence. What these integrating principles are, and how they draw together and unify the various subjects here described, will be fully set forth in the two next chapters; the sole purpose of this chapter is that of acquainting the reader with the courses individually, so that he can at least judge them as constituents.

This curriculum is based, moreover, on three suppositions: one, that the student will have had some slight training in high school in the usual college preparatory subjects, particularly in Latin; another, that once a student has mastered one of the subjects here outlined, he will continue to use it throughout his college career; not feeling that having passed an examination in it, he is through with it. He will continue to use his Latin, for instance, or his mathematics, as they are called for throughout the whole four years. Finally, it is presumed that the student will be given little or no "homework" of the usual kind. At least one of the courses every year will be given at night; this, to habituate every student to using some of his nights each week throughout the rest of his life for profitable study. Naturally, he will be encouraged to make full use of his leisure in reading widely and deeply. But his purely scholastic day will end, ordinarily, with his last class, or at some definite hour toward the end of the afternoon— much as does every working day.

The curriculum about to be presented, therefore, should be judged in the light of all these considerations. So judged, it would hardly seem to be either too varied or too heavy.

FRESHMAN YEAR

Religion. The fundamental dogmas of Christianity, Creation, Original Sin, the Trinity, the Incarnation, the Immaculate Conception, Grace, the Sacraments, the Mystical Body, Baptism of Desire, are to be taken up in accordance with the order suggested by the liturgical year. As each feast occurs, the students are to study the doctrines appropriate to it: the Incarnation at Christmas, the Trinity near Trinity Sunday, and so forth. As far as possible, all the dogmas are to be explained in the words of their greatest saintly expositors, as well as in the words of the pertinent encyclicals.

Practically, this course would encourage the student to contemplate these mysteries of the Faith and to pray, primarily as a member of the Mystical Body. It should also show him very early what is meant by *"laborare est orare."*

Logic. This course would afford training in logic and clear expression, prescribing many exercises in classifying, defining, distinguishing, hypothesizing, judging, comparing, evaluating, experimenting and scientific investigation, and the detecting of fallacies—especially those of propaganda. The student would be trained to dictate, speak, and write a clear, straightforward prose article. The course would also train in the arts of communal discussion (as practiced in the Platonic dialogues) and in the intellectual cooperation required for making a joint report—the arts that gave birth to our Constitution and that presumably are practiced in every conference or symposium.

The course would have a laboratory period during which the instructor could watch his students at work, as does a good teacher of design in an art school.

Latin and Choral Singing. This course would be designed to make the student proficient in the Latin of the Mass, of the Breviary, and of the Vulgate in general. It would concentrate his attention on living Christ throughout the liturgical year, encouraging him to master the Latin language primarily as a means to that end. Students would be trained in Gregorian chant so that, as soon as possible, they might join in singing at least Completorium every day.

Philosophy. This general introductory course (described at length in Chapter V) would be based on the notion that man is here to make things properly, so that through cooperating with God he can make himself fit and ready for enjoying the Beatific Vision. It would therefore show students the major principles of cosmology, psychology, logic, ethics, ontology, aesthetics, as these are all necessarily implied in any act of skillful making, whether it be the making of a tool, an instrument, a machine, an organization, a performance, a life, or, in some sense, a soul. The method of teaching would be experimental, casuistic and Socratic (see Appendix A).

The Art of Studying. In this course, the student would be trained in the arts of reading, memorizing, note-taking, scheduling his work, et cetera. It would not be a full course.

Physical Training. Here the student would be trained to think with and through his body, as do good ballet dancers. He would be trained to master the arts of performing skillfully certain inevitable actions, such as lifting, jumping, tugging, climbing, walking, breathing, running, swimming, throwing, dodging, falling safely, et cetera. He would be shown how to get his exercise in his daily work, being taught how to plough, hammer, saw, stoop, move furniture, sweep, sit at a desk, write, and so forth, properly. No calisthenics will be allowed; but games requiring team-work would be played frequently. There should be some marching and drilling as a company, mainly to assure esprit de corps and ease in parading.

Literature. In this course the student would be trained in discriminating good works of fiction from bad. He would read all types of stories; first, for enjoyment, and then for re-enjoyment through critical evaluation. This latter would consist of checking on each story, factor by factor; he would determine the kind and quality of: its emotional effect; its theme; its plot; its characterization; its background; and its integration. Different evaluations of these factors would form the basis for class discussion. Meanwhile each student would be given the opportunity to try his hand at solving the major problems of fiction writing; this, to give him some appreciation of the technique of fiction and of the difference between a technically perfect but meaningless story and a technically imperfect but profound story. He may discover also whether or not he has any real talent in this kind of writing and be stimulated to develop whatever talent he has; for good Catholic writers of fiction are desperately needed today.

The student must be made keenly aware of the fact that we should be likely to ignore or misprize certain realities unless we had dramatists, poets, novelists, to make us see and appreciate them. He should be shown how the three major codes men live by are persuasively manifested and made hypnotically effective by great literary geniuses: he should be made appreciative of the truth and error in the naturalistic and humanistic pictures of life presented by great writers; and he should be made to feel as well as see and understand how the Catholic picture subsumes, as it were, whatever is good in the other two.

Finally, he should be given some experience here in symbolic exegesis and thinking: going through exercises in allegorical, moral, and anagogical interpretation * both

* The method can be briefly illustrated through its application to the parable of the sower whose enemy sowed cockle among the good seed. Allegorically, this story means that the Devil plants bad people among good; that God permits the bad to exist among the good lest in punishing the bad, He destroy also the good. Anagogically, it refers to what will go on in Heaven at the Last Judgment, when the good will be separated from the bad, and the bad will be punished in Hell (hence, the burning of the cockle). Morally, the story gives us a lesson in tolerance, adjuring us not to persecute even sinners, and not to risk harming the innocent in our desire to punish the wicked.

of fiction and of life—in accordance with the methods suggested by Aquinas in the *Summa,* Dante in his letter to Can Grande, and St. Bonaventure in the *Reductio Artium ad Theologiam.*

The works studied should be drawn, as far as possible, from the literature of all nations and times, so that the student will incidentally be rid of best-seller provincialism and of any tendency to overprize mere phrasing. Since it is assumed that he will develop a taste for literature and go on reading intensively for the rest of his college career, as well as extensively for the rest of his life, he will be required, in this course, to familiarize himself thoroughly with great type-works, those which will enable him to classify any given piece of writing in terms of its main emotional effect, its "message," its plot structure, and its technique of presentation. He should thus be made familiar with the basic forms of tragedy, those of guilt and of failure, as shown typically in Sophocles, Shakespeare, and such a modern as Dostoievsky or Graham Greene; with the two major types of comedy, as shown in Aristophanes and Gilbert and Sullivan, on the one hand, and Molière and Meredith, on the other; with the story of decision, as in Racine, as against the story of adventure or enterprise, as in Stevenson; with the various humorous and non-humorous forms of allegorical or fantastic writing: the Apocalypse; the *Divina Commedia;* many of the tales of Poe and Hawthorne; *Pilgrim's Regress,* by C. S. Lewis. He should learn, in other words, to recognize all kinds and qualities of literature, regardless of time and place: seeing what they are essentially, and appreciating them exactly for what they are, and only incidentally studying them as historical documents or examples of trends in this or that society. Works from all cultures, ages, and levels of quality should be chosen here, so that the student will have something more than a hot-house or academic appreciation of literature, be able to judge things on their merits, not on the degree to which they conform with models or canons of some one era or people.

Mathematics. This science, the key to the formulation of those aspects of things which otherwise escape the grasp of the mind, the instrument of measurement for the inorganic sciences, has many educational values: it provides the purest laboratory experience in the art of reasoning; it shows the wonderful articulation of axioms, postulates, propositions, corollaries; it affords discipline in neatness and accuracy; it trains in detachment; it acquaints students with the "splendor of order"—the beauty of metaphysical quantity, which Plato thought the highest means of purging the soul of sensuality—it prepares students for understanding such concepts as the One (a value) in the Many (its expressions), infinity, and the virtual simplicity of God.

The student, being trained: (1) to discover mathematical truths, (2) to express them beautifully in word, symbol, and diagram, and (3) to apply them, will therewith acquire many skills and many key ideas. He will master enough mechanical draughtsmanship to turn out expository "works of art." He will learn to distinguish the beauty of a proof from that of the phrasing or the visual imagery in which it is presented. He will acquire concepts of time, duration, quantity, space, relationship, order, purity, abstraction, accuracy, simplicity, fixity, boundlessness, universality, uniformity, virtuality, clarity, transcendance, approximation, unity—all of which should provide him with preliminary definitions and analogies for the better understanding of philosophy and theology—for understanding and appreciating the Beauty of Good as the Form of Forms and the wondrousness of the Incarnation of such a Being, through His "emptying Himself" into one form, the human.

The student should be trained to philosophize about Quantity, since mathematics is the philosophy of Quantity, acquiring no truth about a number or a figure without contemplating it in its deepest implications: what it can tell him about how an infinitely pure Spirit thinks, what it can tell him about one of the sets of stencils, so to speak, that God used in creating the world.

The student should also be shown the limitations of mathematical thinking: what the true relations are between Quantity and Quality, why the over-cherishing of numbers, which can be deadly in their fascination, has often misled, not only the ancients, but also the most modern of scientists and philosophers—biologists, logicians, psychologists, metaphysicians, as well as the mathematicians themselves. There are, indeed, so many values in mathematical training that one of the main tasks of a teacher of this subject is that of restraining himself as well as his students from considering it as anything but what it is, namely a single branch of philosophy.

In this course above all it will be wise to teach inductively, heuristically: to aim at helping the student to acquire skill and wisdom rather than knowledge. *Here, as elsewhere, but here particularly, the aim must be to turn out young masters rather than advanced students: young mathematicians rather than graduate students of mathematics.*

The first year, therefore, should be given over to training the student in working out the fundamental concepts of arithmetic, algebra, and geometry; in acquiring the art of formulating mathematical ideas and analyzing mathematical propositions; in mathematical hypothesizing, experimenting, and discovering of implications; and in acquiring the skill to turn out, diagram and all, a solution good enough to be incorporated in a book. The last three years can then be given over to an orderly mastering—not memorizing—of algebra, geometry, analytical geometry, calculus, the goals attained to be determined by the student's abilities.

Crafts. A full explanation and justification of this form of training is given in Chapter V. Suffice it to say here, therefore, that training in crafts is necessary for sharpening the student's cogitative sense, for integrating his heart and head, for enabling him to serve his fellow men with the fullest use of his talents, and *for giving him a deep realization of what is meant by the embodiment of an idea,* and hence for enabling him to appreciate, analogically, Creation and the Incarnation.

Perhaps it is also helpful to explain at this point why the student would best be trained in three crafts: gardening, carpentry, and lettering.

Gardening is to be studied for these reasons. It acquaints the student with the basic form of wealth, the sources of all fundamental productivity. It offers an excellent opportunity for making clear to him the interdependence of all elements and parts of the cosmos. It shows him the whole cosmic cycle of energy. It brings home very forcefully the truth that a craftsman must obey his material, since here forcing it (the land) causes a dustbowl. It brings him into direct contact with the things mentioned by Our Lord in His parables: "A sower went forth to sow . . . By their fruits ye shall know them . . . But an enemy came and sowed cockle . . . Solomon in all his glory was not arrayed like one of these . . . I am the Vine, you are the branches . . ." As Aquinas says, man can make words that stand for things, but only God can make one thing *mean* another; and here are most of the *thing-words* with which He, through His Divine Son, talks to us.

Through his experience in this course, the student will also come to learn that farming is, essentially, not only a means for maintaining personal independence and sound family life, but a prerequisite of social happiness as well— a professional vocation which should fix basic prices by which all other just prices are to be determined, and hence a vocation that is the foundation of all the other vocations. This craft of the earthworker is, in fact, a vital one for any person who would learn to love God and serve his neighbor with utmost Charity.

Carpentry was chosen mainly because it is the craft taught to Our Lord, but also because shelter, like food, is one of the fundamental necessities of life, and because this craft can well represent all the others which (although they too require obedience to material) also imply construction: the clear visualization of a pattern suggested by a very positive and carefully calculated obedience. Carpentry is basic for an understanding of architecture, on the one hand, and cabinet-making, or carving, on the other: it raises all the main problems of mechanical design, and it induces the student to distinguish carefully between the intrinsic beauty of a structure and the extrinsic beauty of its decorative elements, showing him how even a chicken coop can be beautiful both as a shelter and as a word. This craft, too, like that of gardening, will provide the student with a vocabulary of images which should help him to understand, cogitatively, certain philosophic analogies, as well as some of the analogies drawn by Our Lord from building.

The craft of lettering and illuminating has been selected as being an equivocal or transitional one—a craft on the borderline between the communicative and the noncommunicative arts; and because it would have great practical utility, both for the college itself and for many of the students.

As a borderline art, lettering would afford training in general craftsmanship—in such things, for example, as the making of pens, book bindings, et cetera—while at the same time it would introduce the student to the problems of pictorial design—those of effective and pleasant legibility. This craft is particularly valuable in making a student realize how inconspicuous, in the proper sense, all style should be, even the richest; how little any form of expression should call attention either to itself or to its author, its primary purpose being that of enabling someone to appreciate a meaning. The fact that any style of type which calls attention to itself or to its designer is to that extent bad will soon force a student to realize that a medieval architect, sculptor, painter, composer, or poet was right in feeling about his work as does a modern scientist; that to flourish, art needs the same anonymity as does science. A sound course in lettering is an excellent training in humility.

Practically, the course would be of great value because

it would enable the college, at least as time went on, to fill its library shelves with loose-leaf, mechanically reproduced texts (especially patristic texts) which are now unavailable mainly because publishers cannot avoid losing money on them.

The lately developed process of reproducing books photographically may well occasion the rebirth of *scriptoria* —lettering shops—since this form of reproduction can be both less expensive and more beautiful than machine printing. As letterist or type-designer, therefore, it is quite likely that the talented graduate of the course here proposed would be able not only to serve his college, but also to enter an interesting vocation.

SOPHOMORE YEAR

Religion. Christ. In this course, the student will be given an understanding of Christ as the Second Person of the Blessed Trinity; as the Messiah; and as the Redeemer and Head of the Mystical Body; as Founder of the visible, organized Church. All the doctrines taken up previously will be restudied in the light of Christ—as related to and clarified by Him: the Trinity and Christ; Creation and Christ; Original Sin and Christ; and so on. The student will have explained to him just what is meant by "following" Christ and by "living" Him. He will come to appreciate the central position of Christ in dogma, in morals, and in the liturgy.

Greek. This course will be a study of the New Testament, the student mastering the Koiné Greek as an aid thereto. The book used will be, if possible, bi-textual: the Koiné on one side, the Vulgate on the other. Special attention will be given to ethnological and historical facts; but the student will also be given some training in interpreting this book allegorically, morally, and anagogically. Towards the end, he will be given commentaries by the Greek Fathers.

Natural Science. This will be a course in cosmology, using physics and chemistry as subsidiary sciences—they being taught here as the cosmology of immediate, rather than ultimate, causes. The student will be shown how a sound theology is impossible without a sound cosmology; and he will be encouraged to take delight in the wonder and beauty of God's manifestation of His Science and Power through the universe. The student will be helped to master the art of meditation through being given practice in the method of interpretation suggested by St. Bonaventure in the *Reductio Artium ad Theologiam.* He will be shown the limits of common-sense, scientific, and philosophic thinking when it deals with the world about us, and the values of poetic and religious thinking as concordant and supplementary thereto. The relationship of cosmological and artistic principles will be stressed in accordance with the method suggested in the section dealing with the course in technics (see Chapter V). In short, the student will be shown how to recognize and obey the laws of God's Creation so as to be able to cooperate with them effectively and to see God through them as we see a man's character manifested in and through his handwriting.

Psychology. This course will be designed to give the student a clear and practical account of the essential nature of man. It will show how to the question, What is Man? there have been given three answers, the naturalistic, the humanistic, and the Christian; and how the second subsumes the first and the third subsumes the other two. It will show man as a creature seeking his ultimate happiness in God and having his faculties given him for that primary purpose. It will show, therefore, how he comes to know, to will and to feel, so as to adjust himself to nature, to his fellow-man, to himself, and to God. The fundamental doctrine of the course will be that of St. Augustine: *"Thou hast made us for Thyself, O Lord, and restless is our heart until it rest in Thee."* The student will be shown what man might have been in the state of nature, what he is actually, since the Fall and the Redemption, and how to control his faculties and his emotions so as best to regain his integrity and save his soul; this from the point of view of the psychologist. Concretely, he will be taught such things as: the principles of memorizing, those underlying leadership, those of emotional self-control, and those of mental hygiene; those governing the avoidance of sin and the acquisition of virtue.

JUNIOR YEAR

Religion. The Mystical Body. In this course the student will be taught the essential meaning and all the ramifications of this particular doctrine. He will be shown the Christian resolution of the problem of individualism and communitarianism; of authority and liberty; of personality and self-abnegation. He will be shown how Christ extends himself in the Church as a leaven for all individuals and human institutions. The same method will be used here as is used in the course on Christ; *i.e.,* the method of correlative explanation: the Mystical Body and the Trinity; the Mystical Body and the Mass; the Mystical Body and the Sacraments, et cetera. The main purpose will be to show the student what it means to be a member of the Mystical Body of Christ in all the actions of life.

The student will here learn to adopt the right attitude towards the Church, seeing it not only as an instrument for perfecting himself so that he can come into close relations with God as an individual; nor only as an organization with a hierarchy designed to teach and minister to a mass of people called the laity; but also, and primarily, as an organism, a divinely inspired and divinely animated Super-person.

The course will show the student, therefore, how to know the Mystical Body, how to appreciate it, how to be a good member of it, how to cooperate in its growth. It will show him that just as the individual person is a body, an organic federation of members and faculties given life, form, and unity by a soul which can control and can perfect itself by Grace, so the Church is a body, an organic federation of coalescent members and faculties, whose Head is Christ, which, vivified by the Holy Ghost (the Love of God), can feed and train itself and cooperate in the whole work of the Trinity. The student will be shown that the Mystical Body is not, however, exactly an organization, or even an ordinary organism, since its members are more closely bound together sacramentally than are a man's heart and his brain, and yet each member is an independent organism, a whole person who is never merely part of a larger whole. Thereafter, it will be possible to bring home to the student the exceeding beauty of this

Society-Divinized: its unity; its variety (of variously gifted members and nations); its vividness (indefectibility and holiness); its appropriateness (to all times, peoples, needs, purposes). And since these are the criteria both of fullness of being and of beauty, the student will come to appreciate the Church in all the splendor of its Body and Soul.

He will also see how man, in his blind desire for such a Society, has been caught by the humanitarian dream of the Brotherhood of Man, or by the sorry nationalistic equivalent, the Totalitarian State. The course should therefore make the student very grateful for the privilege of being a member of that the very shadow of which seems to most men all they can hope for.

Philosophy. The appreciation of beauty. Here there would be an exhaustive exemplification and explanation of the fact that God is Beauty: that He is the essential Beauty of which all other beauties are, in a sense, a refraction. The primary object of the course is that of training students to detect and enjoy the Splendor of God in all its generous manifestations, and to serve Him and mankind as splendidly as possible. Through previous training in craftsmanship (in purely non-communicative arts such as gardening and carpentry; in semi-communicative arts such as lettering and illuminating; and in essentially communicative arts such as singing and writing) every student will have the basis for an understanding of the beauty of things made; thence it will be easy to lead him to an appreciation of things created and of their Creator as such. The student should come away from this course with sound standards for appreciating any work of craftsmanship or art—from a toothbrush to a "Last Supper"; and

43

he should see quite clearly the relationships of art and wisdom; of art and science; of art and culture; of art and propaganda; of art and liturgy, et cetera. He should be able, indeed, to appreciate fully the exact meaning of such a statement as: *"Ex divina pulchritudine omne esse derivatur."*

(For a fuller discussion of the scope and methods of this course, see also Chapter V.)

Economics. This course would deal with the best methods of supplying man's physical wants charitably as well as justly. Because economics (like medicine) is a science of what ought to be done to keep things normal, the course would show what the normal man—that is, the saint—would do were he concerned with producing, exchanging, and distributing wealth. Then, its norm thus laid out, the instructor could proceed to study the reasons why men fail to live up to this norm, the ways of making it easy for good men to do so in spite of bad men who want to live selfishly, and the best methods for the good men themselves to follow under present and general circumstances. In short, this course would show how men could most charitably satisfy their own needs and those of their neighbors, with no sacrifice of higher values to wealth: no sacrifice of freedom to comfort; of excellence (quality) to efficiency (mass-produced quantity); of mercy to justice (through usury); of happiness to pleasure; of joy in craftsmanship to delight in luxuries; of peace to success; of grace to profits and "a high standard of" animal "living."

Concretely, the course would show the student how to set about transforming all business into a professional system animated by a code of Charity. For this purpose

44

it would use as basic texts such works as Belloc's *The Servile State* and his *The Restoration of Property*; Gill's *Work and Leisure*; Fanfani's *Catholicism, Protestantism and Capitalism*; the pamphlet called *A Declaration of Independents* *; and Penty's *A Guildsman's Interpretation of History*.

The student would also be guided realistically into the choice of a profession or a craft in which he could live both effectively and charitably. As far as possible, he would also be given training in running a credit union, forming a cooperative, et cetera, following the methods already proved effective in Sweden, Denmark, Finland, and especially in Nova Scotia.

The Old Testament. In this course the student would be given the facts necessary for a sound understanding of the life and culture of the Jewish people and some conception of the literary forms in which they expressed themselves. (He would have the experience of writing proverbs, parables, historic incidents, psalms, et cetera, the subject-matters being given him in hint form from passages in the Old Testament.) He would be shown their philosophy of history, as well as the methods for allegorical, moral, and anagogical interpretation. The growth of the messianic tradition would be studied as thoroughly as possible. It would be carefully shown to him in what sense the Old Testament is figurative or prophetic of the New—how the Old Man was tolerated and made ready for redemption. He would be shown how the love of the One God saved Israel—how Charity is the true law of progress.

* Put out by the Distributist League of New England and published by the Sower Press, Scotch Plains, New Jersey.

Christian Courtesy. This course, which might ordinarily be entitled *Ethics,* is one in which the student is taught, primarily by the case-system, not only his rights in Justice and his privileges in Charity, but also how to work out the most decorously kind way of exercising these: how to do the most charitable thing in the most charitable-because-considerate-and-beautiful way. He is to be taught, for example, how to give most effectively, considering such questions as: Is Maimonides right in saying that the highest gift is that of a job got for someone anonymously? the next, the sending of money anonymously? the next, the sending of food and clothing anonymously? et cetera.

The course is based on the idea that Christian courtesy * is the full flowering of Christian Charity in Christian conduct. The so-called primitive people have never forgotten that the best way of doing something—the most satisfying ritual—is almost as important a consideration as the best thing to do: that performing a delicate service grossly is almost as bad as not performing it at all; that every action must be not only good but beautiful before it can be thought wholly true—what it should be. It is time that Catholic students regained this integrity of view; and this course would help them to do so: it would help them to see that the question, *how* must we do this best in Charity, occurs not only when the priest raises aloft the Host, or grasps the Chalice in the prescribed way, but also when a student enters, by chance, the wrong classroom, when he chooses what clothes to wear on his mother's birthday, when, as host, he ushers someone into the house

* Father Ronald Knox, in his recent translation of the New Testament, prefers this word to "modesty" in St. Paul's Epistle to the Philippians. The Douay Version runs: "Let your modesty be known to all men." Father Knox's version: "Give proof to all of courtesy."

or refuses propaganda publications of the Jehovah's Witnesses at the door.

Neither in the search of cases to be analyzed nor in the determination of the principles to be taught would the instructor in this course find much difficulty: the cases could be drawn from the daily life of the students and from biographies of saints; the principles have been exhaustively explored by St. Thomas in the *Summa*.

Biology. The purpose of this course would be three-fold: that of purging the student of evolutionism and mechanism; that of illuminating his previous study of gardening, as well as of casting new light on psychology and preparing him for the course in physiology; and finally, that of getting him familiar at first hand with the actualities of physical life, and especially those of the organism, so that he may thereby acquire in the strict sense, a *real*, rather than a merely verbal, appreciation of what is meant by calling Grace the *life* of the soul and the Mystical Body a Super-organism.

The student should, then, come away from this course thoroughly aware of the stupidity of trying to reduce living things to merely non-living principles; of trying to ignore teleology and design in all things and in the animate kingdoms especially. He should be filled with the wonder of all the adjustments of the cosmos: the mineral to the vegetable; the vegetable to the brute; the brute to men; men to the Supernatural; and all to one another. And he should appreciate intensely what an organism is, as against an organization; what a human soul is, as against a life-principle; and, above all, what is meant by being *incorporated* into the Mystical Body as a *member*.

SENIOR YEAR

Religion. The Mass, the sacraments, and the sacramentals. Since the Mass is the supreme and crowning act of Christian worship—that in which the love of man for God and of God for man gets its fullest and richest expression—it will form the central object of study of the final course in religion.

The Mass is the supreme act of Charity: it comprises all the acts of love and spiritual marriage. It awakens in the Christian heart the desire for union with God, showing him God's might, majesty, lovableness, beauty. It brings home to him his own unworthiness and weakness. It stirs in him a deep gratitude. It provides him with the means of offering both the sacrifice of an humble and a contrite heart and the only Victim worthy of God—His own Son. In return for his own full self-donation, he receives, in a form truly proportionate to his human frailty, the very Gift of God Himself. In all this he is given the privilege of sharing liturgically with his brethren in the graces given to the whole Church. And throughout, he is given the best means of releasing his love: in the most expressive and beautiful utterances and actions possible.

The course would show how the liturgy of each season of the year trained the student's heart especially in one or other movement of Charity: one or other movement of desire for union or of gratitude.

The sacraments and the sacramentals would be studied for themselves and also as preparations for or extensions of the Mass: baptism, for example, being shown to be not only a rite of rectification, but also of the first reception

48

of Christ (Christening), of incorporation into the Mystical Body, and of initiation into all mystical privileges; or the Stations of the Cross being explained in themselves, but also being presented so as to help bring out the full significance and to dispose for a proper reception of the Calvary of the Altar.

And because *lex orandi est lex credendi,* the student would again be given a review of the main dogmas of Christianity.

Politics. Just as economics is the science of the art of being charitable in matters of wealth, so is politics the science of the art of being charitable in matters of justice and peace. It shows men how they *ought* to get along, not simply how they *do* get along, with one another; it shows them how God-loving men would act politically; the spread between that norm and the way in which men do act; and the best methods for reducing that spread.

This course would be given in the fourth year for several reasons: First, because students ought to learn to turn to political means last in solving social problems. Second, because mature political thinking requires quite mature minds. Third, because, using Plato's *Republic* and St. Augustine's *The City of God* and *The Federalist Papers* as texts, students would be continually faced with the problem of immanence and transcendance, which problem is dealt with in this same fourth year in the courses in ontology and natural theology. The student would thus come to realize clearly and keenly the import of such questions as : How near is the City of God to the City of Man? What do we mean when we say, "Thy Kingdom come"? What is the relationship between Justice and what is dispensed in our law courts? What is the relationship be-

49

tween the *vox Dei* and the *vox populi*? What is the relationship between the Mystical Body and the Community of Nations? What, in short, is the relationship between the things that are God's and the things that are Caesar's?

Philosophy. Ontology and natural theology. In these courses, the central problem would be that of immanence and transcendence: the relations of matter to the immaterial, and of the immaterial to the spiritual; of making to creation; of causality to destiny; of the ideal or normal to the actual and the average; of possible worlds to this world; of the scale of being. The student should be taught to wonder at and cherish God's transcendence; and to be grateful for His immediacy and immanence. He should be shown the forms of false mysticism which grow from pantheism and deism and from idealistic perfectionism, or spiritual utopianism.

He should be shown to what extent metaphysics and natural theology have always been dependent on, not to say parasitic on, Revelation and Charity. Through a study of Bonaventure's philosophy here, the student can be made to see how necessary it is to proceed from God to nature as well as from nature to God, being made to see that there never has been anything like a truly independent ontology or natural theology. The former is the science of the *product* of Charity; the latter, of the *style* of Charity: that is, of how the "character" of God shines through (to our intellects) His way of creating and sustaining.

History. The Papacy and Liberalism. Since the Papacy is at once the only central body that has weathered all the storms of our history and the earthly head of the Mystical Body, it alone affords a proper object for a truly revealing study of European and American history. It alone gives students the opportunity to see worldly affairs as they actually do take place, and yet see them *sub specie aeternitatis*. Through this study, the student should come to see how those who would be animated solely by the love for God and for neighbor must needs live in the world and not of it; that the Mystical Body itself has suffered more than one Passion through the weakness of some of its members within and the many cruelties of its foes without; that for all the faults of its members, this Body itself is flawless, without spot or wrinkle: the Bride of Christ. With the Papacy thus the major object of study, it will be inevitable that humanitarian liberalism—the enemy to all mysticism—will become the minor object of study, the antitheme. From this study, there should come a clear sense of the statement, "My Kingdom is not of this world," and of the love-born heroism that is always likely to be required of every true Catholic. No student leaving such a course should feel that only in warfare will he be granted the privilege of knightly heroism; for, as this history will show, the cause of Charity is always in danger, sometimes even from those who should be its best defenders. He will learn that if he wishes to show his love for God in action, there are always dragons to kill for that love.

Physiology. The main purpose of this course is that of ridding students of any lingering puritanism they may have about their bodies. It would therefore show them how beautifully functional these are; how amazingly well articulated; how, without Body-Beautiful sentimentality, they can be regarded as being informed by an immortal soul so as to show forth the nature of that soul. The course should so acquaint the students of it with the truth, goodness, and beauty of the highest of God's physical creatures, that they can never thereafter regard it with shame, but only themselves, for not using it properly in the service of God. The course should, in fact, enable students to see their bodies as doctors, biologists, saints see them, substituting mature appreciation for childish prudery.

Naturally, this study should have practical values as well; it should give an insight into the fundamentals of hygiene, enabling the student to use his physical powers to their greatest advantage; at the very least, making easy the work of whatever physicians he may need to consult throughout his life, and freeing him from the nonsense of self-medication and quackery.

To summarize this curriculum briefly, therefore, we may say that it is one which is designed to train students to live fully effective Christian lives. Consequently, it is made up of those subjects required for that end, and of no others: it is "limited," that is, to the arts required for being a truly living member of the Mystical Body and for following a vocation charitably. Its courses are arranged as an athletic coach or a master craftsman would arrange them: so that the student will learn fundamentals as soon as possible and master the fine points (along with the science they imply) year by year, as he goes along. Since the student is a person, not a mere mind-and-body, and all true action is, as Aquinas says, not of any one faculty or set of faculties, but "of the person," the courses here have been chosen and arranged not only to train his powers of attention, of perception, of judgment, of imagination, of reasoning, and of willing, each more or less separately, but also to make heart, head, and hand all cooperate as organs of the soul.

52

CHAPTER FOUR

INTEGRATION

CHARITY

A CURRICULUM, as we have already had occasion to observe, is never to be considered merely as a collection of studies; it is rather a confederation of them, a quasi-organism, all the studies, like the organs of a body, co-operating to achieve the final ends of the institution while each individually achieves its own ends. It follows, as a consequence of this condition, that the curriculum just described cannot be fully understood (and hence properly judged) until it is viewed in the light of its suitability to the final ends of the Catholic college. We must estimate whether or not each subject and the course as a whole leads primarily to the fostering of Charity and secondarily to the fostering of skill. For a Catholic curriculum is ultimately what it should be to just the extent to which it inspires its students with the love of God and then trains them to act in accordance with that love as effectively as possible.

The present chapter, therefore, will be devoted to showing how the studies proposed in the previous chapter can and must be integrated in terms of Charity. This done, the next chapter will be devoted to showing how most of these studies can also be simultaneously given a minor integration, in terms of skill. Both these chapters, in other words, will be given over to showing how these subjects can be so used, so integrated, as to turn students (as far as they can be turned) into young men both saintly and professional.

What, then, is this Charity which the curriculum must have as its primary object and its central principle of integration? How is it to be awakened and inspired? Hence, how is the college to be determined by it?

The task of answering these questions seems at first sight very difficult. In fact, however, it is not. What makes it seem difficult is the necessity for exercising a little courage—the courage to go for guidance not to the almost highest, but to the highest, sources; for one of these at least seems, in these strangely puritanical days, a little strange, a little hard to take. These sources are: Our Lord Himself and the Canticle of Canticles.

Our Lord has shown us and told us what kind of love Charity is: to Whom it is directed and how intensely. The Canticle of Canticles, that work cherished by the great saints of all ages, suggests to us what love itself is.

For Our Lord has told us, explicitly and emphatically, that the leading motive of life is love; that we must love God with our *whole* hearts, our *whole* minds, and our *whole* souls, and our neighbor as ourselves. He has gone, indeed, much further than that: He has established a "new commandment," bidding us love one another as He loves us.

And by including in the Bible the Canticle of Canticles, the Church has brought home to all its children the fact that if we would try to understand what we mean by love for God, we can well begin by studying and analyzing that which is analogical to it, namely, the feeling of the lover for his beloved. For here, as everywhere else, the law holds true, that Grace assimilates and completes, but does not destroy, nature; so that from an analysis of natural love, we can easily rise, by analogy, to an appreciation of the supernatural. We shall thus be able the better to waken this supernatural love in students and tend it properly, the more we know about the growth of natural love, since the supernatural, though superior to the natural, parallels it closely.

What, then, are the main characteristics of human love at its most intense? How is it awakened, how fostered, how given fullest expression?

The answers to these questions will become quite clear if we outline and analyze the typical, or normal, love-affair; that is, if we study it genetically——from its budding to its full flowering. If we do so, we shall find that it goes through two main stages: the first, that of desire for union; the second, that of an overwhelming gratitude.

In the first of these stages, the lover is brought to appreciate keenly his lack of self-sufficiency, his incompleteness. He comes to realize that his beloved, and she alone, will satisfy him——that she alone "will make his life complete." Thereupon, his desire for union so as to achieve this completion becomes for a time the main motive of his life.

He then sets out to win her. He tries to please her by becoming what she would like him to *be,* as well as by doing what she wants him to do. He works and studies to identify himself with her; to become as much what she is as possible; to live one life with her; to make her interests his own, and to guide himself by these primarily.

During this period he comes to feel how unworthy he is, and to appreciate keenly how much of a favor it would be—— how great would be his undeserved good fortune——if she should ever grant him her love. His unworthiness, the wonderfulness of her possible yielding——these considerations affect him profoundly; so that when he does finally gain her favor, he is swept by a gratitude that turns his original desire into a merely secondary motive: he now becomes more interested in giving than in receiving; and her gifts to him only increase his joyful gratitude. His purest delight then becomes that of undertaking great risks and burdens for her sake, in a knightly spirit. He casts about for all kinds of means to express his love, which grows in that very expression. It is then that the final stage is reached; for it is then that both the lover and the beloved attain the fullest satisfaction of the two desires of love—the desire to be one with and the desire to give, the desire to dominate and the desire to submit. For at this point each person receives fully, gains full completion from, the other by an intensely grateful and joyful self-donation. Through a selfless yielding, each receives a reward far beyond anything that selfishness could ever attain. And the joy of this reward sets going once more the cycle of love: it is followed by an increase in the desire for union and by an increase in gratitude. And so on, over and over again.

From this analysis, then, it becomes apparent that if we are to awaken, foster, and make fruitful in a student an intense love of God, we shall find it necessary to:

(1) Awaken the desire for union with God.
(2) Intensify that desire.
(3) Help him to identify himself with God and make God's interests his interests.
(4) Transform his desire into gratitude.
(5) Intensify this by enabling and encouraging him to give it full expression.

Now, it is obvious that if we are to accomplish the first of these purposes, namely, that of awakening in the student a desire for union with God, we must make the student feel: how wonderfully "satisfying"—how much more than satisfying—God is; how great is the student's need of Him; how much hope he can have that God will graciously answer that need. The steps here, in fact, are simply those of all ordinary persuasion: first, that of making a person feel a need; second, that of showing him what will best answer it; and third, that of showing him how easily he can acquire what will answer it.

In any proper training these steps will not, of course, be taken separately; the student's wonder at, his hunger for, and his hope in God will be roused from the first day of his studies on. But for purposes of orderly consideration, it may be well for us to take them up in the sequence mentioned.

First, then, a student can be made especially aware of his need for God by being shown, through the study of psychology (or, rather, of a psychology that deals with man in action as well as in essence) and of the social sciences and history (particularly Bible history), as well as through training in crafts and through ascetic practices, just how insufficient to himself is he and every other man. For his psychology should show him that he is a creature lacking in integrity and perverse, yet motivated by an unquenchable thirst for peace in the enjoyment of infinite Truth, Goodness, and Beauty—which are to be found in God alone. From dynamic psychology he will learn just how sick the mind can become if its perversity is not kept under control, just as from logic he will similarly learn how prone he is to fallacious thinking. Economics, politics,

history, the great tragic writings, the great satirical come-
dies—all will show these things, proving, directly or by implication, that men who rely on themselves alone are
doomed to bewilderment, despair, bitterness, at the dis-
asters they bring down upon their own heads. The crafts
will show him how great a spread there is between what
he hopes to do and what he can do—how hard it is even
to obey himself. And if he is given the opportunity to
teach others to acquire a technique—as he should be—he
will soon learn how many of his pupil's difficulties are
purely moral, how much leadership is required simply to
persuade a pupil to do only what he knows he ought to do:
make mistakes without trying to excuse himself; take
correction in the right spirit, humbly; hold himself to
doing the work as he ought to do it, and so on. Finally,
the truth of man's dependence, of his disintegrity, of his
need for guidance and grace will be brought home fully
and explicitly when, in the religion course, he is instructed
in the doctrine of Original Sin, while he will be reminded
of it and induced to meditate upon it daily by his various
religious practices. Indeed, every kind of training and almost every course can awaken him, if only incidentally,
to a keen appreciation of man's sorry needfulness.

So, too, can all forms of training be used, on the other
hand, to sharpen the student's sense of the superabundant
"adequacy" of God. They can all make clear to him just
how truly God is the answer to his boundless hunger and
thirst for infinite Truth, Goodness, and Beauty, as they
can all, at the same time, help him attain the Godlikeness
that will enable him to appreciate better and better whatever he learns about God. Properly taught, all the sciences
on up through ontology, all the arts—all studies, in fact—

can serve to awaken in the student a profound awe at the Science, the Skill, the Power of God. If the teacher of physics, for example, will but approach his class with the correct attitude, namely, that of a person who, in loving awe of his Master, and in affection for his students, wishes to show them the marvels of God's ingenuity and power, he can teach them not only what things they must keep in mind if they ever invent or if they wish to study nature deeply, but also how amazing, how awe-inspiring must He be Who tossed this universe off by a mere thought and has kept it going by the mere light of His Radiance. If a student stands in awe of a magician who pulls a rabbit apparently from nowhere, how much more should he be, and can he be, made to stand in awe of One Who pulled the universe from nowhere; for while it is possible to explain the magic of the magician, it is never possible to explain satisfactorily the infinitely more wonderful and mysterious magic of God. And a good teacher of physics, of chemistry, of biology, or of mathematics can so present his subject as to bring home to his students at all times much more than the truths of his science; he can make them realize the startling beauty of this Creation in which these truths are manifested and of the Creator of Whose Beauty theirs is only a kind of refraction. Psychology also can be so taught that the student can feel, with Hamlet, what a wonderfully wrought creature man is:

> . . . how noble in reason! how infinite in faculty! in form and moving how express and admirable! in action how like an angel! in apprehension how like a god! the beauty of the world! . . .

Further, as the student advances in mastery of crafts, he will become more and more reverential of masters of these, more and more appreciative of "good work" and of all men who turn it out; with the result that he can easily be led to marvel at the most perfect making, that which transcends all human making no matter how great the genius behind it, namely, Creation. And if he sees in the various achievements of men in all fields, if he sees that even in making tragic mistakes, men still betray the grandeur which comes from their being in the image and likeness of God, a student will perforce find himself struck by the splendor of God's superabundant Genius, of which all human geniuses are but infinitesimal replicas. Thus all the praise of mankind which otherwise might lead to the arrogance of Pelagianism—of false self-reliance—can, through a proper regard for man's dependence on God, be used to suggest the glory of a Creator Who could make such a creature. To the wonder evoked by nature, especially as this nature is known through the sciences; to the wonder evoked by man and by the arts of civilization as his achievements; to these can be added the wonder evoked by the angelic realm and the far greater wonder evoked by the Mysteries of the Faith, as this is excited by the explanations of cosmology and theology and given expression in prayer, especially liturgical prayer. Wonder, admiration, awe, loving reverence, adoration—all can be prompted, now one, now the other, by the various sciences, arts, and religious practices that should make up any sound curriculum.

Arts, as well as ascetic practices, also serve to increase a student's appreciativeness through helping to make him God-like enough to appreciate, far better than he might otherwise do, the super-eminence of his Master; for the greater the maker, the greater his appreciation of the Creator; and the greater the saint, the greater his appreciation of the Holy One.

To prevent the student from despairing, as do some learned men, of ever achieving union with such a God (for, say they, how could an infinitely perfect Spirit deign to concern Himself with the particular and petty affairs of sordid humanity?), to waken in him the hope implied by the desire for union, it will be necessary for us to stress, if only lightly, the natural goodness of man even as a creature in the state of nature and even in his fallen state—as can easily be done through a study of Adam—and then go on to examine his titles of redemption: *coadjutor Dei,* Member of the Mystical Body, co-heir with Christ, and so on. He can be shown that he must love himself because God loves him; that he has a right to glory humbly in the fact that God sent His Only Begotten Son to redeem and dignify his human nature; that he can be an apprentice to Christ in the Guild of the World; that God respects him enough to let him make his own mistakes, as do few men; that he is never alone, unaided, abandoned. And throughout all his training in dogma and in liturgy, he can be encouraged to acquire the supernatural virtue of Hope, especially through a realization that God is Love Itself.

The transforming of the desire for union thus roused into gratitude will require that the student be given:

(1) A full appreciation of man's sinfulness—not merely of his creatureliness.

(2) A full appreciation of God's graciousness.

(3) A full opportunity and training to release the gratitude which the student feels on attaining these
appreciations.

(4) A full appreciation of each particular favor that he
has received from God.

The appreciation of man's sinfulness will be no more
difficult to give than will the appreciation of his mere
creaturely dependence and inadequacy. All history, and
especially Bible history, can be cited to prove that men are
not saints. The great tragedies, especially the Greek, give
ample evidence of man's perversity and the horribleness
of sin. Dogma and liturgy stress the fact, both directly
and by implication; the sacraments are sufficient signs in
themselves of the same thing. In many courses, therefore,
every student can have forcefully brought to his attention
how unworthy all men (he being no exception) are of the
favor of redemption: there will be no need for a special
course to bring out this truth.

That God should be willing to go beyond justice to the
fullest exercise of mercy for such a creature as man will,
of course, be a strong stimulus to gratitude; but this feeling
can be intensified by showing just how gracious God has
been in thus forgiving and welcoming back His prodigal.
This end can be attained in all courses by a continuous
reference, by explicit statement or hint, to the fact that all
things are free gifts—graces—from God. Not only does He
give the inexhaustibly wonderful universe and the powers
of understanding it and using it; but He also ties only
one string to His gift—and this string turns out to be
none at all. He merely requires us, as a true Father, to
obey Him for our own good, compelling us in nothing.

His very "disciplining" is not for any satisfaction of His
—He does not need our obedience—but only for our own
happiness. God's generosity, therefore, in giving the universe, with all its truth, goodness, and beauty; in trusting
us to use it properly with no interference from Him; in
affording us redemption for our own abuse of it and of
ourselves; and in providing us with His own guidance and
Personal sustenance through the Church, the Eucharist,
and the other means of grace; above all, in rewarding us
with Himself in the Beatific Vision; all these facts can
be so presented in all courses as to become motives for an
overwhelming gratitude to Him. The student for whom
each new discovery is but one more expression of God's
love must sooner or later find his heart burning with
gratitude; for love cannot resist Love.

The student's gratefulness and intense acknowledgment
of God's goodness will be further increased, to his increased joy, if he be challenged with the full opportunity
of serving God heroically, in a spirit of Christian chivalry,
being shown how much there is to be done in establishing
the Kingdom of God on earth—how much skill and charity
he can spend in serving God through serving friends,
neighbors, himself, and his enemies. Through his study of
sciences like economics and politics he can be made keenly
aware of how much yet remains (despite our apparent
progress) for all Christians to do: how much enmity,
how many snares, how many dangers, they must still ride
out against; and, at the same time, how best they may
acquire the arts needed in dealing with these. All the arts,
all the sciences, can be presented as things to master for the
full expression of one's gratitude to God, such expression
to take the form of using all one's talents in charitably

combating the evils of this world. Outside as well as inside classrooms, in helping conduct the affairs of the college and in establishing Catholic centers of instruction and personal aid, the student should be encouraged to ask, "What is the value of this principle or method in enabling me to serve, as well as appreciate, God? How can I use it in serving others? How can I teach it to others?" In sum, he should be shown how to be heroic: how, that is, to live up to the full requirements of a vocation, leading at all times a dedicated life of Charity.

His gratitude should further be fostered by his being trained from the outset to perform the highest acts of spiritual service—prayer, contemplation, the Mass—with the deepest possible understanding, skill, and love. He must be shown how to serve God whole-heartedly and beautifully in the best of all ways—those devised by God Himself working in and through His Church. The student must be taught to participate as intimately as possible in the Mass, one in mind and heart at all times with the celebrant and with the other members of the Mystical Body, the congregation; to be happy in such privileges as responding, chanting, singing, walking in procession; exalted and strengthened by joining in the continuous prayers of the Universal Church through reading the Breviary and chanting, at least once a day, in community. He must have the joy of showing his love for God appropriately, spiritual season by spiritual season, throughout the liturgical year. For as the Mass is, in short compass, an experience of all the stages of love, so is the liturgical year an experience in large, of these same stages. The student can be made grateful at all times; and he can be trained to express that gratitude freely and actively—

happy through being able "to do something for" a Person he loves and to do this as beautifully as possible.

In summary, then: the Catholic college should have and can have as its main motive the awakening, fostering, intensifying, and making fruitful of the student's Charity. In such an institution, all the training should be aimed at rousing his deep-lying desire for union with God and teaching him to achieve this union through contemplation and zealous service of God and neighbor. His whole education will take form from these needs. All the arts and sciences will conduce to one all-encompassing end, that of enabling him to live abundantly through obeying the highest law of man's nature as explained by Our Lord, the law of Love.

CHAPTER FIVE

INTEGRATION

SKILL

THE PRIMARY INTEGRATION of the curriculum is, then, as we have just seen, in terms of Charity. But there is also a secondary integration, ancillary to this first, in terms of skill. For a curriculum must show students how to live, not only charitably, but *as charitably as possible*.

The fact that most, if not all, of the courses in our curriculum can be given this secondary integration in terms of skill should be obvious from the very definition of art in its broadest sense and from the fact that even today, although our colleges should more properly be called colleges of sciences, we still call them colleges of arts. For the word *art,* in its original and broadest sense, means "skill in making or performing." All studies in every college are supposed to lead to the acquisition of this or that skill; and all studies in liberal arts colleges are supposed to have as their integrating aim the acquisition of skill as such, the skill which, to quote Cardinal Newman, "prepares him to fill any post with credit, and to master any subject with facility."

To determine, therefore, how this end can be attained, to discover how the proposed course in technics can serve to give a secondary integration to the curriculum, let us consider closely what the major doctrines of such a course would be, as well as how it could call upon, tie together, and vivify all the other courses.

Now the first and central doctrine of a proper course in technics * is that *all* art is essentially one—all the arts are essentially alike. Whether they are fine arts or applied arts, they are all forms of skill in making or performing.

The second major doctrine of the course is that all making is determined by four factors and the laws governing their relationships; which four factors are:

(1) *Purpose:*

Nothing is made without a purpose.
No purpose: no thing; different purpose: different thing.

(2) *Pattern:*

All things are made in accordance with blueprints, or designs. No pattern: no thing; different pattern: different thing.

(3) *Material:*

Everything is what its matter allows it to be. No matter: no thing; different matter: different thing.

(4) *Instrument (or technique):*

All things are limited by their technical source. No instrument (or technique): no thing; different instrument (or technique): different thing.

Another way of stating this doctrine is this: The proper

* The course here described is not mere wishful thinking: it has been given by the author, in one form or another, at three different institutions.

making of anything depends upon a correct understanding and control, by the maker, of these factors:

(1) The function which the thing is to fulfill.
(2) The form which the thing must have in order to fulfill that function.
(3) The material which is to be given that form.
(4) The instrument and technique required for causing the material to assume the form. (Under this heading, it may also be necessary to consider the *general* social and economic factors: the relationship of maker to patron, and of both to society.)

Still other ways of stating the doctrine are:

(a) Have the right purpose, pattern, material, and technical instrumentation—and you have a successful job.
(b) Have the wrong purpose, *or* the wrong pattern, *or* the wrong material *or* the wrong technical instrumentation—and you have, to that extent, a poor job.

The course can be thought of, then, as raising and answering all the fundamental questions concerning these inevitable factors and the laws governing them, as they determine the making of: a product; a tool or machine; a symbol; an institution or a society; an individual life; and a communal life.

Inasmuch as these factors and the laws governing them are the subject-matters of special sciences and departments of philosophy, the student soon finds these subjects "feeding into" and being harmonized by this general study of technics, which is to the arts and even to the philosophic disciplines what, in a sense, cosmology is to the sciences. Just as a boy, in making a radio-set, masters many principles of physics, so a college man, in gaining an understanding of all forms of making, acquires a synoptic view of cosmology, psychology, logic, ethics, aesthetics, metaphysics, and natural theology. Moreover, in a course in technics, the student deals with things, facts, and laws before he memorizes the names for them: he acquires his wisdom realistically, not nominally.

The lessons are arranged in accordance with the principle that knowledge is best acquired by first "getting a good general idea" of a thing and then refining and broadening that idea, beginning with simple and obvious examples and ending with subtle and complex ones. He is shown, at the outset, how to analyze the making of an arrow or a spoon; and from this he learns to recognize and obey the fundamental principles governing all making. He then proceeds systematically through the thinking of mechanical invention, of persuasion, of fine art, of business, of scientific discovery, and of contemplation.

The course is based on the notion that it is desirable for the student to consider ultimate, as well as immediate, concepts, axioms, and principles. The student comes to see that to know matter thoroughly, for instance, he must view it not simply as the chemist or the physicist knows it, but also as the cosmologist does. To understand thoroughly the main instrument of all production, man, the student is impelled to study him not merely as the psychologist does, but also as the ethician and the metaphysician do. To appreciate the factor of form properly, the student must know something of the difference between image and concept, the particular and the universal—hence, something of logic, epistemology: the theories of criteriology that stem from Platonic idealism, Aristotelian realism, Cartesianism, pragmatism. To know the factor of purpose thoroughly, he must have some understanding of the whole great argument about teleology—about the reality of Final Causes—as well as that about functionalism in industrial design and architecture. Thus the student comes to see that all the philosophic disciplines have a direct bearing on his daily life.

The cosmological problems which the student inevitably encounters are fundamental, being, in fact, essentially those which are taken up fully in the cosmology course (Sophomore Year). He has to decide what the sound craftsman and scientist means by such terms as Matter, Form, Substance, Change. He has to answer the whole great question of how one body can influence another. He is called upon to deal with such questions, to cite a few typical ones, as these:

What is the difference between matter and raw material? Is there such a thing as pure matter, as pure raw material? Has every material thing its rights, so that it cannot be truly imposed on? Does not the scientific craftsman need to obey his material in order to control it? Is movement ever transferred from one object to another—or is not the power of the second object to move simply awakened by the impact of the first? Is movement a quality that can be shifted from one thing to another—is heat? If the maker has to obey his materials, is the universe a republic of substances, each with its own disposition which must be respected, "persuaded"?

Is matter knowable directly? Are the forms of matter? What is the material factor in an event? How does one test out matter technically, so as to be able to say with certainty, "This is an ideal matter for my purposes?"

If matter is energy, is energy matter? Can energy be a raw material? What is matter, as such?

Was there ever a pure, propertyless matter that of itself took on a simple form first, and then gradually, more and more complex forms? Is $\infty \times 0 = 1$ a picture of the act of the creation of the universe? If matter is the fundamental reality, why can a physical impossibility determine a physical possibility?—why can $\sqrt{-1}$ affect the making of machines?

How does the raw material for a thesis happen to be called that? What is the raw material of a painting: the ideas it embodies? the pigment? both?

Directly and indirectly, many psychological truths are brought home to the student in this course. He masters the psychology of skill, learning to distinguish clearly between knowing how a thing is done and knowing how to do it. He discovers that in the work of the professional technician, quite as much as in that of the purely speculative scientist, there is great need for moral qualities: for humility, detachment, honesty, humane self-sacrifice, love of perfection, cooperativeness. He comes to experience the joy of responsible creative thinking; and he sees and feels how necessary to man is the happiness of an enthusiastic and dedicated use of his will and intellect. "The slave does what he has to in his working time and what he wants to in his spare time; the freeman does what he wants to in his working time and what he has to in his spare time."

Inevitably, of course, the student is trained in practical logic, being thus made especially appreciative of his regular course in this subject (Freshman Year). He has to practice defining and classifying his purposes, designs, materials, techniques and processes. He discovers the limitations of analysis—of failing to realize that a thing is always greater than the sum of its parts, like Humpty-Dumpty. His training in analytic experimentation is thus completed by a training in synthetic experimentation: he finds that every maker is a scientist also: to devise a working-model, he must guess (hypothesize) its four causes and try (experiment) to determine which forms of these combine best to produce the particular object he is making. For artist and scientist meet here: the first is interested in the question, How does one control and combine the causes of this thing? and the other is interested in the question, How does one distinguish the causes, separately, that together make this thing what it is? To a man like Leonardo, indeed, there seemed no reason why one should not ask and answer both these types of question at will.

Further, the student would receive much training in the making of sound analogies, a training that is well-nigh invaluable; for an inestimable amount of thinking is vitiated because thinkers cannot make such analogies. In economics, for instance, man is often dealt with as if he were a machine or a commodity. In the fine arts, we have the Academicians slavishly warping their techniques, in a falsely analogical imitation of former masterpieces which had different materials, techniques and purposes from their own; and the Independents are in not much better case, since, in their blindness, they merely react against the Academicians. So, too, for Conservatives and Liberals in politics; for Essentialists and Progressivists in education; for Traditionalists and Modernists in architecture.

In religion, false analogies lead to anthropomorphism on the one hand and to various kinds of Manicheanism on the other.

Not the least valuable effect of the course results from the fact that the student has to learn to think in terms of four variables at once; for he soon realizes that he cannot modify one causal factor without affecting the other three. If he changes his material, he must also change the instrument used on it, modify his blue-print, alter his aim. And so for the other causes. Hence the student, made vividly aware of this co-variation of essentials, attains common-sense, intellectual common-sense.

The ethical questions raised in the course are of great importance, being types of those studied later in the ethics and economics courses (Junior Year) and the politics (Senior Year). To cite only a few of them: Since man, as man, is a creature of free will and intellect, who should find in his work the joy of using these faculties properly, should not conditions be changed so that all men may have the responsibilities, the satisfactions, and the joy of craftsmanship? Is freedom in a democracy merely what Plato said it was—the opportunity to lead an aimless life in going from one pleasure to another? Is it either efficient or just to mechanize human beings, bribing them to perform brute drudgery by promising them luxuries and dissipations? Do we not rather believe that even the lowest forms of manual labor are still arts— that if, for instance, $25,000 were offered annually for the best-dug trench of a certain length and depth, people would soon discover how much of an art ditch-digging is? Is it not true that "an artist is not a special kind of man; but every man is a special kind of artist?" Is not a true culture one in which the joy of personal active creation is considered a precious human right? Does not the real justification for private property lie in the need felt by the craftsman for absolute control of his material and instruments, without which he could never make things as well as they should be made?

Do we want a pseudo-civilization made up of scientists and technicians under the thumb of selfish money-makers whom the public, in turn, put under the thumb of ideological politicians? Or, do we want a civilization made up of artists in investigation, who discover the truth scientifically; artists in production, who use these discoveries in scientifically furnishing mankind with needed goods; artists in exchange, who scientifically make these goods available to all economically; and artists in the assuring of justice and peace, who supervise their fellows wisely? If we wish this second form of civilization, must we not make sure that every man understands what it means to be a scientific artist in his field—that all men have a philosophy of technology in common and share the same responsibilities and joys of technical achievement?

The course offers an excellent introduction to aesthetics (given formally in the Junior Year), since the best way in which to refine one's discrimination and taste is to start with appreciating the relative perfection of ordinary things that have been well made. This, for the reason that there are only three kinds of beauty: the beauty of appearance; the beauty of nature; and the beauty of the symbolic significance; and if one knows the nature of a thing so as to appreciate the perfection of that nature, then one finds it easy to appreciate the appearance and the symbolic value of that thing. The man who knows the nature of an anchor, who understands how it is determined by certain functions, a certain pattern, material, and manufacturing process, can doubly appreciate the appearance of an anchor and can easily see how fittingly this instrument is used as a symbol of hope and security.

The student here learns that a thing well made cannot help being beautiful, to anyone who sees its perfection. Beauty is not a cosmetic plastered on to tickle the sense; it is the splendor of intrinsic perfection which is mainly perceived by the intellect; and it is just as truly, though not as richly, present in a well built typewriter as it is in the Taj Mahal; in a good map or blue-print as in Botticelli's "Birth of Venus"; in a good theorem as in the *Divina Commedia*. The man who learns to appreciate the one can readily learn to appreciate the other. He needs only to train himself to recognize the perfection of any kind of achievement to sense its beauty. For truth, goodness, and beauty are but aspects of perfection: when we say, "There's a real job!" we also mean, "There's a good job!" and, "There's a beautiful job!"

It is obvious that this course will serve as an excellent introduction to ontology (Senior Year), since it has many metaphysical implications, only a few of which need be noted here. The prime requisite for all sound metaphysical thinking is that the mind should discern the unity and the diversity of being. All things are one in having being; but each thing is a distinct kind of being. The great fault in philosophizing is that of trying to explain all kinds of being in terms of some one finite form of it. If, for example, one presumes to explain all reality in terms of "ideal" being, as if it must have only such qualities as ideas have, and strictly defined ideas at that, so that all

75

things must be thought of as evolving in a purely dialectic fashion, one falls into the proud intellectual stupidity of idealism and rationalism: one becomes too rational to be reasonable. If the ideas by which one measures all reality are purely mathematical, one falls into what has been called mathematicism. Or if one believes that God is the only reality, one falls into theologism, pantheism, occasionalism . . .

Now, a student trained in the course here proposed would be well immunized against this sort of error. He learns that all things are alike in having four causes, but that each thing has its own particular four causes and therefore is, in a sense, unique. He is not simply told this; he comes to feel it. No one who sees a general creative method prove of value in one field after another can doubt the unity of being; and no one who sees the modifications of that method that are necessitated in each new field can doubt the diversity of beings. He cannot help absorbing the sound philosophic attitude toward the One and the Many. And he acquires first-hand knowledge of the problem of the universals: seeing that the idea in the mind of a maker is a kind of *universale ante rem*; the idea embodied in the thing, a *universale in re*; and the idea in the mind of an inspector or appreciator, a *universale post rem*. He is made ready for understanding all the fundamental distinctions of philosophy: essence-existence; potency-actuality; substance-accident; cause-occasion, and so on.

A consideration of the problems of natural theology (those dealt with systematically in the Senior Year course) would be prompted by the student's inevitable question: If particular things have a maker, a plan, a purpose, has not the universe as a whole? He cannot help being interested in God as a Supreme Artist, and in trying, by analogy, to determine His nature from His handiwork. He also faces the problem of determining in what sense man is a co-operator with God. He may ask himself if evil can be viewed as the non-Godlikeness of nature and whether it is not his task at least partly to remedy that condition. He may even learn to understand and appreciate the value of contemplation.

This course, then, should make the student aware of the fact that he is no mere Economic Factor, Social Unit, or Thinking Machine, but a Scientific Craftsman—a Man, each of whose actions can be interpreted fully by no one science alone, but only by a sound philosophy in the light of all the sciences and of common-sense as well. The student should find here the pattern whereby he can correlate all his experiences in terms of a virtue that is both intellectual and moral, the virtue of Prudence. He should be brought to feel that it is practical to be wise and wise to be practical. And he should come to understand and rejoice in his position in the world as a free agent, intelligent and responsible, skilful and honorable —at once scientist and artist.

The final value of this training, in fact, will not be so much intellectual as moral and spiritual; it will develop skills, but above all it will develop natural and supernatural virtues. The student will learn what it is to make things not only prudently, chastely, thoroughly, and thoughtfully, but also Charitably. This, as a result of two facts: first, every maker is himself "made" by his action of making; and second, the same principles which apply to the making and operating of a physical thing apply, analogically, to the "making" and "operating" of the Christian soul.

For when any craftsman sets out to do "a good job," he soon discovers that he cannot succeed unless he exercises the virtues required for such work. If he is imprudent and conceited, he will try to do something well beyond his ability—and fail. If he is intemperate, he will go in for unnecessary and absurd virtuosity; or do only what he needs for getting the money wherewith to satisfy his various lusts. If he is lacking in fortitude, he will work impatiently, irritably, lazily, finishing nothing. If he is proud, he will turn out what will gain applause, whether it is good work or not. On the other hand, every time he acts humbly, he confirms himself in humility; every time he acts patiently, he confirms himself in his habit of patience, and so for the other virtues; since virtues are, after all, only moral habits, and all habits are strengthened by repetition. Virtues are required in making things just as much as they are required in conducting oneself; or, if you prefer, craftsmanship is a form of virtuous conduct, which, like every other form, confirms the very virtues it requires.

No virtue: no true craftsmanship. So certain is this, that the Guilds came into existence primarily to assure the moral conditions that are a prerequisite of good work; their main task was that of assuring that apprentices should become not marvels of skill, cold-blooded and selfish experts, but masters who sought to act justly, unselfishly, devotedly, humbly, and charitably.

For the Guildsmen realized that, *other things being equal, the saint would always turn out better works than the sinner.* They saw that the argument that a loose-living genius can produce greater works of art than a pious booby is beside the point; just as much beside the point as is the contention that piety automatically and inevitably produces talent. For the point at issue is this: does the debauchee with a certain talent produce art as good as he would produce with that same talent were he a saint? Merely raising the question is enough to suggest the answer; and no student who had had sound technical training would fail to realize this fact.*

Far above the purely moral values of this training in philosophically grounded technology will be the spiritual. Craftsmanship proves a beautiful handmaiden to religion because it enables the student to do well whatever he ought to do, thus permitting him to be charitable in the quality as well as in the kind of things he does. For, first, it increases his love for God by enabling him to appreciate God's Beauty—training him to appreciate the Beauty of the Uncreated by observing its reflection in things made and in things created. Second, craftsmanship inspires the student to express his gratitude to the All-Perfect fittingly, making and doing all things as perfectly, hence as beautifully, as he can. Third, it enables the student to draw others to God, soliciting them by lovely act or sign or symbol to contemplate and serve Him.

The course in technics should, in fact, prove an agency in integrating not only the secular courses, but also the

---

* But, may come the objection, a saint would never eat, dream, and sleep an art, as some artists do. Hence he could never achieve what they achieve. Possibly—although a monomaniac, even when he has genius, is not likely to have the most profound things to say. Then, too, there is the question: Have we a right to ask for an excellence that is attained at the price of possible damnation?

spiritual. For craftsmanship provides the student with the means for understanding and appreciating this "valley of soul-making" (to use the phrase of Keats). For just as every craftsman learns that for its full functioning, he must make sure that his product will be conserved, protected, and properly operated, so will the Christian craftsman learn by analogy how, for its full functioning, he must feed his soul, protect it, and operate it in Charity. Through a prudent mastery of art, the student will thus arrive at an artistic fulfilment of prudence, doing all things with the excellence of Charity.

CHAPTER SIX

THE TEACHER

I

IF A TEACHER IS, in the general sense of the term, an artist, he will obviously be a good or bad one to just the extent to which he realizes: (1) what his true purposes are; (2) what the nature of his material is; (3) what the form is into which he wishes to "cast" that material; (4) what technique is best for doing so; and (5) what skill and good will he must exercise in acquiring that technique. So far, we have considered the first three of these questions, determining that (1) since the end of all activity for the Catholic is Charity, the prime object of Catholic education is the training in Charity which will help the student to live as charitably as possible both in college and out. We have also noted (2) that the "material" on which the Catholic college teacher is to exercise his skill will be a boy who as a Freshman will be no older than fifteen or sixteen: a person in the image and likeness of God, who yet, because of creatureliness, as well as original and accumulated sin, needs especially to have trained not only his intellect, his will, and his memory, but also his cogitative sense—that faculty by which he gains skill in perceiving the universal as it is embodied in the particular and in applying universal principles tactfully, resourcefully, as he deals with particular problems and invents particular devices, plans, and methods. We have seen (3) what form the boy is to take—into what "pattern" this "material" is to be "cast" if it is to fulfill its functions properly. We have concluded that the Catholic student should come forth from his training a professional craftsman inspired to lead a truly charitable life as a member of the Mystical Body of Christ.

These determinants having been fixed upon, the questions which arise next are these: What are the principles by which the teacher in a Catholic college must guide himself? What kind of person ought he himself to be? How should he train himself and keep himself in training?

Since he will be primarily occupied with the art of teaching an art in a religious way, it is fairly clear what he must *not* be. He must not be uncharitable, worldly, ambitious, unresourceful, unimaginative, uncraftsmanly, set in his ways, school-marmish, vain, narrow, opinionated, intolerant, tactless, insensitive, tasteless, dowdy, fussy, slovenly in dress, prim, or precious: he must not be, that is, an incarnate contradiction of the principles he advocates. Technically, he is not to be defined as an investigator who gives lectures and corrects blue-books. Certainly, he must not be the typical Master of Arts or Doctor of Philosophy; for the typical Master of Arts is, in fact, master of no art; and the typical Doctor of Philosophy is seldom what his title signifies (literally, "a teacher of the love of Wisdom"), since he knows neither how to teach nor, as he would admit, how to distinguish knowledge from Wisdom: he does not, in all honesty, believe that Wisdom can even be found, to say nothing of its being taught.

82

The teacher in the Catholic college must rather look upon himself as a master and a foster-father—as, at the very least, a kind of Knute Rockne of the mind and soul. Coach, master, captain and foster-father, he must see his task as that of training his students, not that of stuffing them: as that of making sure he always knows the state of their bodies, of their minds, and of their souls—their "condition"—the state of their skill and their morale; as that of feeding out his information as needed, not before; as that of being able to demonstrate, as well as analyze and talk about, the technique he wishes them to acquire; as that of leading them: gaining their trust and affection, curbing them, consoling them, inspiring them. The physical, the mental, the moral, the spiritual—all their needs are in his care.

He should know how much and what kind of training to give to the powers of knowing, of cogitating, of willing, and of acting; at the very least, avoiding the fallacies into which people commonly fall in regard to such training. He should realize, for instance, that his work is intensive rather than extensive; that because he is primarily concerned with the developing of habits (but even if he were not), learning is, in a sense, mainly up to the students themselves (the proportion of learning to teaching being as seventy-five to twenty-five) since it requires hard work to make the mind properly receptive; that students should be encouraged to learn methods and absorb facts rather than learn facts and absorb methods,*

* The student of chemistry, for instance, should learn *how to make a chemical discovery himself*—not merely how to *repeat* classic experiments or *recall* their results; and so should he learn to philosophize, not memorize philosophy; classify and define, not merely memorize laws of classification and definition; et cetera.

and that, consequently, there must be at least sixty percent practice to forty percent theory; that his work is more supervisory than explanatory and disciplinary; in brief, that he must deal with his students as good masters have always dealt with their apprentices.

He should be keenly aware of the fact that learning about an object or about how something is done is one thing, whereas learning how to do something is quite another; and that, because he is primarily concerned with the latter, he cannot adopt the theories or methods of teachers who disregard these distinctions. He cannot act upon such commonly held assumptions as: that knowledge is power (for any book-worm can turn his mind into a useless curiosity shop or fill it with instrumental concepts he does not know how to use); or, again, that as each precept is handed out by a teacher "in logical order," regardless of the student's technical needs at the moment, it automatically generates the skill necessary for either appreciating its value or for putting it to effective use (as if by simply showing a student what a definition or a classification, for example, looked like, the teacher was infecting him overnight with the habit of turning out flawless definitions and systems of classification); or, yet again, that memorizing is better than the familiarizing which results from acquiring information with some clearly defined purpose in mind; or, in line with this last, that it is better to turn out great memorizers than good thinkers.

The good teacher of an art should be specially sensible of the absurdity and harmfulness of a marking system based on the delusion that it is possible to judge skill by testing a student's memory of facts and formulae.

Nor is anything more ridiculous than the practice of marking a student at the very outset on a skill that he is setting forth to acquire, and then, at the end of the year, averaging in his early marks with his latest. This is much like forming one's final estimate of a man like Pasteur partly on the basis of the marks he was given in elementary chemistry. Further, it is very unwise to encourage a student to overprize marks: instead of finding out what things he cannot do well and spending extra effort on these, he will often relax into doing what he can already do well, being assured thereby of "good marks." Moreover, if an intellectual tortoise sees himself being outstripped by the intellectual hare in his class; if the poor plodder sees that his swift-footed friend always gets higher records, he may lose heart and drop out entirely; whereas if he is not discouraged by his early slow progress, if he is not easily thrown off balance by the sight of a few D's, he may go on to conquer fabulously. It is a rash teacher indeed who would dare say how much skill any student will have acquired by the day after tomorrow. And the assumption that marks can be relied on to indicate either at just what moment a student will acquire a knack or which knack he can be expected to acquire is as unfair to the student as it should be patently absurd to the teacher.

But perhaps the most dangerous, though indirect, result of following the system of marking now in general favor is *the destruction of the sense of leisure which is a vital condition for any efficient study*. The unfortunate student who is made to feel that he must "cover the ground," that he cannot drop behind for a minute, is so worried that (as he would say) he cannot think straight.

The irony is that he cannot do so because he is too worried; if he were not worried, if he had a proper sense of leisure, he would cover the ground easily. His plight, inconceivable to the ancient Greek, in whose language the word for school is the same as the word for leisure, results from the exigency that the teacher, in order to mark frequently, has to subdivide his matter into small units which the student must assimilate on the dot; this despite the fact that every teacher should take into account the slowness of maturation, plateaux of learning, sudden insights, emotional blocks. Student and teacher alike, once they have given their homage to the over-lord Marks, sooner or later find themselves his slaves—all leisure, all freedom, all human ease, all joy in learning dispelled by the horrible sputtering of his pen as he fills in the Record Sheets, the *Liber Vitæ* of the modern world.

All these fallacies, which arise from teaching an art as if it were a mere body of information, will of course never mislead a teacher who sees clearly what the acquiring of an art means: one who understands what the normal stages of making something or of performing something are; hence who sees what the normal stages of training for these actions must be and what dispositions of mind and of heart must be assured.

Thus, in "bringing a student along," the good teacher will be mindful of the fact that, in acquiring any skill, a student will go through these several stages: First, that during which he is mainly concerned with "familiarizing" himself with the general purposes, the materials, and the instruments of the given art; the point here being that the student be rendered free of apprentice fear, through so trying out the instruments and materials and estimating experimentally what they can and cannot be expected to do, that he come to "feel at home" with them. The next stage is that during which he clarifies, brings into quite sharp focus, his exact intentions: just what functions that which he is making—whether thing or performance—must fulfill: what effects it is to have; what needs it is to meet. Then he must visualize what, as a consequence of these needs, the *general* specifications of the thing must be: what qualities it must have in order to do what it is supposed to do. After that, he must learn how to explore the possibilities of his materials: exactly what they will and will not do. Next he must make many tentative working models, "mock-ups," *esquisses,* or rehearsals. Then he must invent, on his own as far as possible, the technique required, asking for guidance only when he needs it, and consulting others, especially the great masters as they speak dimly through their works, only when, as a result of honest failure or part success, he is ready and anxious to profit by what they have to tell him. Naturally, as we have already noted (in Chapter IV) the student will begin to make whole things, performing whole operations (however small each of these may have to be) at once, refining his skill in dealing with the four factors as he proceeds: in making the first few things, giving most of his attention to familiarizing himself with materials and instruments; in making the next few, giving most of his attention to defining and clarifying purposes; then, in making the next few, giving most of his attention to testing out materials thoroughly; and so on: at all times making wholes and thinking in terms of all determinants, while giving special attention, at this or that period, to this or that determinant.

Meanwhile, the teacher will be specially mindful of the following general principles of craftsmanship and pedagogy:

(1) *Technique follows intention*: the man who knows just what he wants to do, and is anxious enough to do it, will learn how to do it, in spite of almost any obstacle.

(2) *We learn best what we learn for ourselves, on our own:* a student must not be encouraged either to imitate the solutions of others or to adopt unthinkingly their methods.

(3) *The student should be given guidance only when he feels the need for it and asks for it;* but he should of course be taught, by unsparing but tactful criticism, never to be content with amateurish work, no matter if it is good as home-work: he should learn to develop and hold to his own standards; and they should be high.

(4) *The teacher should almost never "take over" and show the student how to finish or perfect anything:* the teacher may point out a defect and discuss the principle involved in it, even showing how a great master followed the right principle in dealing with a similar problem; but no teacher should permit himself to do a student's experimenting or accomplishing for him.

(5) *The teacher must, indeed, encourage the student to instruct others and himself:* * the student must be given the opportunity to teach others, both for his own sake

* For an understanding and appreciation of these all too commonly neglected principles the writer is deeply indebted to a very great teacher of painting, the late Charles H. Woodbury. See his works, *The Art of Seeing* (Scribner's) and *Painting and the Personal Equation* (Houghton Mifflin).

and for theirs. For his own sake because teaching is a very profitable method of learning, and because through it he learns to become his own guide in technical matters, his own critic and master. He must master teaching for the sake of others, since all through life he will be teaching them: as a master training apprentices; as a father bringing up children; as a member of the "royal priesthood" of Christ (which includes the laity) in edifying those not yet of Christ's kingdom.

Along with principles, the teacher must keep in mind certain common misconceptions held by most students, being especially on guard against these: the ambiguous notion that any action is "easier said than done"; the apparently sound objection of the student who says, "But surely no poet or experimenter or contemplater ever thought of all these rules you have been handing out when he sat down to compose or analyze or test out or contemplate"; the unfortunate superstition, acquired through years of mis-education, that it is necessary to have a special talent for this or that work; that if you have one talent, you cannot have another (there being something abnormal about being good in both mathematics and literature, for instance); and that unless a thing can be done well, as only a man of special talent can hope to do it, that thing should not be done at all, or even attempted.

The wise teacher of an art must clear away the first of these delusions (that things are easier said than done), or he will be likely to find it paralyzing his class. The misconception here is both dangerous and easy to explain away. For if a student really believes that the words "easier said than done" mean easier *described* than done, he is naturally liable to despair, since analysis and formulation in abstract terms can make even the simplest of actions seem appallingly difficult to anyone who has not performed that action. Witness how difficult it is to describe what takes place when the organs of speech produce the sounds "Dada," and how easy it is for a baby to produce them! If an instructor fails to warn his students against taking a complex, and often merely academic, formula as the equivalent of the action it defines, he will do more to prevent the student from learning than he will to aid him in learning. He will be a bogeyman, bewildered that he is not looked on as a foster-father.

If the teacher does quickly dispel this first delusion, he can then the more easily dispel that which goes with it; namely, the notion that because great artists in any field quite obviously do not "think of" the principles of logic, rhetoric, philosophy, et cetera, as these are set forth in textbooks or in lectures, at the moment when they are arguing or composing or philosophizing, therefore the thing to do is treat these principles as speculatively interesting and go on to memorize facts, rely on imitation, and trust to talent and hard work. The teacher can dispel this delusion by showing that, although at the moment of obeying the right principles, these men were not adverting to them deliberately, saying to themselves, "Now I'll use this form of syllogism, or that kind of metonymy, or this method of negative transcendance," still, unless they had learned how to obey the right principles automatically, as a matter of second-nature, they would not have been able to analyze, compose, or philosophize as effectively as they have been. It is easy, in fact, for a teacher to make this point clear if he will use an analogy drawn from a sport, such as football. For it is obvious that a forward-passer does not, at the very moment of making a pass, "think of" all the principles he obeys in executing this play; but it is just as obvious that the better he knew them and the more he was habituated to them, the better would be his passing. It is for the teacher, then, to show his students, by this and other analogies, what the thinking of skilled action is: that it cannot be coldly deliberate, merely conscious; nor can it be wholly instinctive and *un*conscious; it must be both intentional and *sub*conscious. The ability to think thus is the result of the conscious refinement of instinctive action, along with the practice that makes its performance a matter of habit. The man of skill does "without thinking" what he can do only after a great deal of thought and practice.

On the other hand, the teacher who analyzes, abstractly and speculatively, *from without,* the performances, works, or discoveries of great artists and, having hit upon certain purely academic formulae, then makes his students memorize these and obey them slavishly (Great English writers use many words derived from Anglo-Saxon; great logicians begin by defining their terms; therefore you must always do the same)—such a teacher either destroys whatever powers of cogitation his students may have or so disgusts them with all "theory" that they reject even vital principles when they come upon them.

No less harmful, at the other extreme, is the so-called inspirational teacher—he who, having "inspired" his students with hazy visions of grandiose projects, leaves them to the task of working out for themselves the methods for carrying these projects through—leading them on with flattery into a false trust of their talents, and dodging

recriminations by admitting (with a great show of intellectual humility) that, after all, education is in the end a
very mysterious business . . . no one can really teach
an art . . . one can't make a silk purse out of a sow's
ear . . . and look at the preparation the students get
these days! . . .

That teacher, then, who belongs to neither of these
classes, who is neither academic nor inspirational, is the
only one who can teach an art as an art; for he alone
understands and can make his students understand the
difference between an essential principle and an academic
formula; and he alone can show a student how to practice so as to develop intellectually founded habits.

He, too, is the only kind of teacher who can rid students of the third set of delusions mentioned earlier,
namely: that everything requires a special kind of talent;
that if you have one kind, you cannot have another; and
that there is no point in trying to do anything unless one
can do it as well as the man with the special kind of talent. For a good teacher of an art knows that if so-called
primitive Indians see no reason why a man should not
be able to ride, compose war-dances, be a good archer,
canoe, fashion good clothing, make up songs, and the like,
neither should we see any reason why a civilized man
should not be able to master these or similar arts. It is
natural for all men to learn a language, to reckon, to
compose music; we have forgotten that fact only because
we see one man do one of these things better than another—so much better that what he produces seems to
belong to a special order of things unattainable by the
rest of us. And students contracting this view from their
elders, especially from their teachers, soon fall into the

despair of those who think that because they can do nothing supremely well, they can do nothing at all. But the wise teacher, understanding that an art is still an art even when it is not a fine art, can raise students from their despondency by showing them that though they may not have the genius of Shakespeare, of Beethoven, of Michael Angelo, of Pascal, or of Aquinas, they have all the abilities (in however unexercised a condition) of all these men.

Another tendency with which the teacher in a Catholic college must be prepared to deal is that which is sometimes called verbalism but might better be called imagism and conventional apriorism: the tendency to think in terms of a few images, blue-prints, conventional formulae, and rubber-stamp judgments rather than in terms of things experienced freshly and honestly, as well as judged freshly and honestly.

The good teacher must realize how common is the vice of translating words or concepts into some image or diagram and then dealing with this rather than with the reality to which it refers. Unless the teacher does realize the hold which this vice has on many minds today, he will not be able to train students to deal with things or truths either practically or speculatively; for the ordinary student, even the extraordinary student, is usually so great a slave to his not too exact images of things, that he finds it very difficult to see past them to what they stand for, and act accordingly. As a case in point: suppose a faculty adviser suggests to the editors of the college weekly newspaper that they change it over into a weekly magazine. What happens? The students immediately translate the words "a weekly magazine" into a picture of some weekly magazine or weekly magazines with which they are acquainted: they see it as *necessarily* comprising an editorial page, several regular features, a poem or two, articles of not more than fifteen hundred words, perhaps a cartoon. Then, when they try to put out such a publication, they find they cannot live up to its requirements. Instead of determining what kind of magazine they should be producing, they attempt to turn out something well beyond their powers, with the result that the best writing in college never gets printed and the editors waste their time sweating out amateurish imitations of professional work. Were they trained to think first of the broadest possible meaning of the words, "a weekly magazine," then of the best form of it possible under the given conditions, and only at long last (and then merely for hints) of the existing magazines, they might turn out a publication which, although it did not look like *Life, Liberty,* or *The Commonweal,* would interest readers because it contained the best writing available. The fact that their magazine did not resemble the first image to be brought to mind by the word "magazine" would not trouble such editors: what if the issue of one week contained only one long article on a topic of interest that could not be discussed in a short article, and the issue of another week contained an editorial, a sonnet, a book review, and two articles?—these might still constitute magazines far superior to the merely correct. So, too, in other matters requiring practical action. Hence the expert teacher will try always to detect and deal immediately with this form of imagism.

The vice must also be taken into account in purely

speculative matters. Perhaps the hardest person on earth to educate is the one who assumes that your definitions are necessarily his, and vice versa: the student who assumes that he "knows all about" what you are referring to when he has translated casually your words into his own imagery or into that which is commonly adopted by popularizers, newspaper experts, or best-seller experts. Say to such a person, for example, that "teaching is a difficult art," and he will immediately presume that you must mean: "Teaching, because it requires years of scholarship and because the teacher must deal with students who are generally moronic, is a process of lecturing, disciplining, and testing; hence it is very arduous and boring"; whereas you might be intending to suggest that "teaching, an art concerned with a very mysterious material, namely man, requires that its practitioner possess not only great skill, but a keen sense of values and a profound enthusiasm that spring from fervent Charity; hence it is never to be thought of as a process of mere lecturing, disciplining, and testing." Your listener, smugly complacent in the belief that he knows exactly what you cannot help meaning, makes it impossible for you to explain to him what you do mean; this, even when you warn him of the dangers of misunderstanding you and go out of your way to dispel his presumptions. Similarly, when a person of this kind reads a book, he comes away thoroughly convinced that he has understood what the author has said when, in fact, he has misunderstood, mistranslated, and mis-valued every major term in it.

The teacher, then, who overprizes ideas, cherishing them for their own sakes and failing to keep in touch with the realities whence they were derived, is in grave danger not

95

only of mis-preparing his students for action and specula-
tion, but also of encouraging them in their callow glibness.
Unless a teacher makes his students deal directly and
honestly with a fact before they either formulate the truth
about it or accept the common valuation of it, he will turn
out wise fools; parlor-pundits who know all the names
for things they have not seen, all the formulae for truths
they do not understand, and all the evaluations of these
truths except their own. Whoever permits a student to
talk about a mystical ecstasy as if he had experienced one;
or about *Coriolanus* as if he had seen it when, in fact, he
had read what is but the scenario of the play; or to discuss jurisprudence when he had never been in a court-
room, or to talk Christology when he had never read
Christ's life carefully, or to try to discuss the Mystical
Body when he could not give an adequate definition of an
organism—whoever permits a student to indulge in such
glibness hardly deserves the name of teacher: his students
are those almost unbearable creatures, the Permanent
Sophomores. He is equally no teacher if he encourages, or
even permits, his students to adopt uncritically either the
time-honored verdicts—the lip-service—of the past or the
fashionable condemnation—the de-bunking bunk—of the
present. His concern must not be to make students memorize accepted judgments about books they have never
read thoroughly, pictures they have seen only in photo-
graphic "black-face," symphonies they have heard on the
radio once, philosophic theories they do not even begin to
understand, et cetera; his concern must be to make them
acknowledge honestly at all times just what they know
and do not know, and just how important or unimportant
every doctrine seems to them, and why. He must make

them develop true discrimination and exercise it honestly —humbly admitting, for example, that although they see reasons why *The Merry Wives of Windsor* might well seem extraordinarily funny to others, it does not seem very funny to them; or that Dopey in the Disney version of "Snow White" seems to them a much more pathetically lovable character than any in Shakespeare; for obviously, it is only when students admit things like this honestly and humbly that the instructor can help them to see why others—like Coleridge, perhaps—do disagree with them. A good teacher prefers turning out an honest rough diamond to developing a synthetic pearl.*

It hardly needs to be stressed, of course, that the good teacher must do more than avoid the fallacies in the way of sound intellectual training; obviously, he must know the positive principles of learning as well; and not only

---

* Perhaps the doctrine of the last few pages can best be summarized in the following burst of song:

THE MISGUIDED STUDENT

There once was a student who erred:
When he studied a thing, he preferred
To take a good look
At the thing, not a book.
A queer—Oh, a very queer—bird!

His teachers all said, "How absurd!
Poor lad, he seems not to have heard
That a thing is just real,
While a thought is ideal,
And better than both is a word!

"Alas, what a shame! what a shame!
He'll never succeed at this game:
He is wasting his youth
In a hunt for the Truth,
And all that we ask is its name!"

know them but steer by them. He should, that is, order his course with reference to such principles as the following (to cite only a few) :

(1) No student should be admonished to concentrate or to make a positive effort to strive: this admonition only leads to his concentrating on concentrating or on striving, not on getting anything done.

(2) A student should be encouraged to deal with wholes, aim at whole accomplishments and master whole tasks, before he deals with parts. For instance: he should be required to read his texts *through* as soon as possible, and often.

(3) He should be encouraged to correlate every new item he acquires with his existing fund of knowledge, using here the laws of association, but also fitting it into some over-all system of belief, seeing how it supports, modifies, destroys some theory or set of theories in various fields.

(4) The student should be taught to over-learn; that is, he should be taught to go over a thing several times after he has decided that he has "got it."

(5) He must be encouraged to familiarize himself with a subject rather than try to memorize it: just as he comes to "know" his friends, so does he come to know a subject—by associating with it, so to speak, in friendly interest, intimately, continually, absorbently. The expert never memorizes consciously; he absorbs.

(6) He must be given, and encouraged to find for himself, as many opportunities for teaching subjects as possible: the best way in which to crystallize knowledge is to pass it on to others: man retains by giving.* Obedience

* The value of such training, to say nothing of its economy, has already been amply demonstrated by the late Professor Butrus M.

to these and similar principles of pedagogy is, then, the
minimum requirement for any teacher.

But more important than the teacher's ability to deal
with the student's powers of knowing is his ability to deal
with the student's powers of willing. The teacher must be
something of a psychiatrist—he must know something
about mental quirks and ills—and something of a leader.

As a mind doctor, he must know how to win the student's affection and confidence; to know the student well
enough to detect when something "is wrong" not only
with his soul but also with his mind. He must be familiar
with the writing of such men as T. V. Moore and Rudolf
Allers; so as to be able to detect, or at least make a fair
guess about, what lies behind the laziness, or exhibitionism,
or defensiveness, or shyness of his students, and what
measures he should take in helping the student eliminate
these faults: how to make the always late student reform
by appointing him as taker of attendance, and so on. The
teacher should be able to distinguish between what is apparently wrong with a student and what is really wrong

---

Maluf, a great Syrian educator. In the small town of Mashrah, Syria,
he established a one-teacher college by the simple and surprisingly
effective expedient of starting in with a class of primary grade students and giving his better students the chance to teach whatever they
themselves had mastered. As a good student was graduated from one
grade to another, he was permitted, under supervision, to teach a class
or tutor individuals in a subject, or a part of a subject, in which he
had excelled. As time went on, Professor Maluf's "General College"
became what its name implies: an institution of elementary, inter-
mediary, and advanced study, higher and higher subjects being incorporated into the curriculum as the students advanced in learning—
the older students of competence doing a good part of the teaching of
the younger, all under the supervision and instruction of one man.
That the experiment was sound is proved by the fact that the school
produced many more brilliant graduates than do institutions of greater
resources.

with him (they are seldom identical) and modify his treatment accordingly, knowing when to "go easy on" a student and when not; when to put him on his own, when not. As a doctor, he must know the case history of his patient and adapt his regimen to his patient's needs wisely and sympathetically.

Since he will be but one among several teachers, he must be able (or rather anxious) to cooperate, in Charity, with them in a coordinated treatment of each student, subordinating his own desires or interests to those of the student, which can best be served by the whole faculty working together. He will thus not try to make the student spend, let us say, many extra hours on Greek when the student needs to devote special effort to his mathematics, or vice versa; he will rather adhere to some common agreement about how much time each student individually should be giving at this or that moment to each of his subjects. All his cases will be consultation cases.

In short, a teacher must be a master of all the arts of sound tutoring and coaching.

II

So IMPORTANT is it that a teacher be a master of leadership, of guidance, and of inspiration, as well as an expert in explaining, that it is necessary that he should be studied particularly under this aspect; for we are all too prone to forget how much greatness is expected of him (and rightly expected of him) as a leader and inspirer of mankind.

This requirement has been commonly overlooked because students, parents, and teachers alike have come to adopt a narrow view of what a student is supposed to be doing. Being a student has come to mean: listening to lectures, doing home-work, reciting, and taking written tests—all for the gaining of "credits." Once we adopt the right view of education, however, we see that it is a process quite different from this—a process, in fact, aimed more at the development of wisdom than at the acquisition of knowledge. For, in the right view, it is seen to be a series of practice periods—not class hours—during which students willingly submit to making fools of themselves before their fellows, betraying their awkwardness and ineptitude, in mastering difficult arts like those of controversy, experimentation, speaking, singing, giving a meditation— all for the sake of serving God at the moment and of preparing to serve Him heroically later on in a world in which they will continue to look like "fools for Christ's sake."

Seen thus, the process of education appears very much like a process of spiritual military training. Without question, it calls for leadership. It follows, therefore, that the teacher in a Catholic college must know what this requirement means and the best way of meeting it.

The very least that he can be expected to know here— a least too often overlooked—are the rules and principles which must be followed if there is to be any true leadership at all. He must see them as resulting from the two main purposes of leadership, which are: negatively, to prevent students from suffering any kind of paralyzing discouragement; and, positively, to make them courageous, humbly aggressive, and charitably enthusiastic, both as individuals and as members of a team—here, the "team" of all teams, the Mystical Body, the Church Militant. The teacher must make his students capable, largely through his subleadership under Christ, of using all their natural talent, skill, and resourcefulness to the utmost; so that they will be able to withstand the physical, mental, and moral shocks of life and go on, undiscouraged, living a full life of Christian peace and Charity.

The good teacher knows how to accomplish his first general purpose, that of preventing his men from losing heart, because he understands the causes and conditions which naturally lead even strong men to "lose their heads." By and large, these factors are neither very complex nor very subtle; they can all be put under one general heading: anything which prevents a man from judging, reasoning and willing normally. Specifically, such factors may be reduced to the physical, namely weakness; and the mental, namely bewilderment. Timidity and tension are the two great enemies of skill: a student who is too weak or too bewildered to think straight is at the mercy of his instincts: he can neither think nor act effectively; certainly, he can develop little or no skill.

For if anything is true of human nature, it is these three facts:

First, that man must exercise continuous control over his powers, through reasoned decisions and well-formed habits, or those powers will get out of hand.

Second, that it takes energy, poise, and peace to think clearly and act normally on one's own—especially in doing an unaccustomed thing, such as acquiring a new technique.

Third, that it is therefore very easy for a nervous (weakened) or bewildered man to be, as it were, hypnotized into following unthinkingly his strongest impulses, even when he is sure in his heart that they are the wrong impulses.

These three fundamental facts are founded on a still deeper fact, namely, that man is a federation of powers, or minor selves, each of which tends to act—because of Original Sin—on its own, and all of which have to be kept in line. A man is either an army of faculties, well-disciplined and controlled by his conscience and reason, or he is a mob of faculties, ill-disciplined and controlled by his passions and impulses. And since it takes energy and will-power—to say nothing of grace—for him to discipline and control his powers, it is easy for a man to be a mob and difficult for him to be an army. It is only through sound deliberation and good habits that man assures the team-play among his faculties which is necessary for unified, coordinated action.

The Catholic teacher will hardly need to have this truth defended or dwelt on at length; but he will do well to keep in mind certain manifestations of it as studied by experimenters in abnormal psychology; for these will give him the key to certain problems in instruction and leadership which he might otherwise find almost insoluble.

Experimenters in abnormal psychology have discovered that when patients suffer from catalepsy, which renders them incapable of both thinking and willing normally, they obey instinctively suggestions which are given to them from without. Let the experimenter stand before the cataleptic and raise his right arm, and the patient will automatically follow suit; that is, the patient will automatically raise his left arm—as if he were following an image in a mirror. Or let the experimenter form the patient's hand into a fist, and the patient will gradually and automatically assume the posture of a prizefighter.

And what is true of the cataleptic is only a little less true of hysterical and extremely nervous patients. These are intelligent enough to *understand* suggestions, but under certain conditions they too find it extremely difficult to resist them. The cataleptic neither understands nor resists; the nervous person understands and may even feel like rebelling, but finds it difficult to do so.

Similarly, even the normal person who has momentarily, through weariness or anxiety, been reduced to the level of the nervous patient, finds resistance to his own obsessions and to external suggestions very difficult. The weary subway rider can hardly help yawning when he sees a fellow-passenger across the aisle doing so. And anyone trying hard to learn how to ride a bicycle makes straight for the nearest lamp-post because his fear renders him so open to suggestion that he concentrates on what he should *not* do—and proceeds to obey *that* suggestion. His anxiety has so paralyzed his reason and his will that he can obey only what his senses and his imagination suggest most powerfully to him. Ironically enough, the strongest image which these faculties present to his mind is that of the very action his higher faculties do not want him to perform. He visualizes so clearly the action of riding straight at the lamp-post which he is anxious to avoid that he cannot keep himself from running into it.

Once a student's powers of self-control have been weakened, then, his inferior powers take over; and these latter are likely to obey the strongest instinct or habit that is awakened at that moment by some inner or outer suggestion: some memory, some fear, or some outer movement.

Clearly, therefore, one of the main abilities which a teacher must possess is that of preventing his students from falling prey to hypnotically paralyzing uncertainty, anxiety, or discouragement. As far as possible, the teacher must make it easy for every student to act with the confidence required for success. And since, to act in this spirit, a student must know that his action is to be, in general and in particular,

> morally justifiable (good),
> effective (true),
> and glorious (beautiful),

the first task of the teacher is to make sure that the student does not look upon his action as

> spiritually insignificant or wrong,
> ineffective,
> or inglorious.

He can accomplish this twofold purpose of eliminating anxiety and of inspiring a vital confidence by making a student sure of himself, sure of his training, sure of his fellow-students, sure of his teachers, and sure of his cause.

The student can be made properly sure of himself, first of all, by being properly trained physically; for it is of prime importance that he possess that extra energy without which he will not be able to think clearly, quickly, and calmly. His physical training must therefore be such as

(1) develops great energy and powers of endurance;

(2) develops ease in executing the movements required by the main labors of life;

(3) develops the habit of acting thoughtfully *at all times*.

These requirements flow naturally from the necessity for being able (1) to withstand shock; (2) to summon energy quickly, on call; (3) to adapt oneself to new and startling postures, obstacles, or tasks; (4) to maintain complete control—reasoned and deliberate control—over one's whole person at all times, so as to assure the physical attitude of poise, confidence, and grace that enhances and makes easy the adoption of the proper mental attitudes.

All these considerations imply that the student should never indulge in mere—that is, in unintelligent—exercise; he should never allow *any* of his faculties or organs to be doing one thing while his mind as a whole is doing something else. He must never lose sight of the need for psycho-physical coordination—body-mind integrity. He must learn, indeed, to control his body and his mind as a unit; somewhat as a general controls his various services: he must train them to act together harmoniously, *purposely*. For this reason, he should be required to play games that require energy, skill, and poise all at once: games of subtle team-work, of fair complexity, of some toughness; since he must be forced to deal with situations requiring vigorous action, quick thinking, the ability to maintain poise even under strain and pressure.

No less important than such games are exercises in the mastery of such tasks as are encountered every day: climbing fences, jumping creeks, moving furniture, sweeping, and so forth.

The student should not be subjected to calisthenics. For in these he is not told to perform movements with any clearly recognized purpose as well as pattern in mind; he merely learns to move about without any purpose—unintelligently. Or, what is worse, he may come to think that stiff, staccato, jerky exercise, setting one muscle against another, exercise in which he almost yanks himself out of joint, is the only kind that will assure strength and grace. The truth is, of course, that here as everywhere else, development largely takes care of itself when things are done with the right intention. If the student is trained to move purposefully and yet as easily as possible, all the ends of physical education will be gained: he will develop the strength he needs; he will acquire ease and grace; he will attain the physical poise that is conducive to mental. Without conceit, he will learn to be confident of himself as one "who can take it" and can put his physical powers at the disposal of his mental and spiritual.

Just as a student must repose due trust in his bodily powers, so must he repose due trust in his skill and in his character. To this end, the teacher must assign work in proportion to the student's ability, and he must make the student aware, by a careful marking off of each new stage in the student's progress, of just what things have been done, just what skill has been mastered, just how professional and competent the student has become. Assignments should be clear-cut; the student should know exactly what he is to do; and all vagueness that begets fear should be dispelled. The student should be shown by the teacher's natural respect for his ability and by the evidence of his own accomplishments that he must be a person of some skill.

Throughout all his training, in fact, he should feel inspired by the Christian encouragement that he receives. We all like to believe in ourselves; as St. Bernard insists, in his work on the steps of humility, we *must* believe in ourselves; but being mysteries to ourselves, we are never quite sure whether we are really worthy of encouragement and of respect until we are given them by outsiders—especially by those whose judgment we believe to be exact. Consequently, it is a necessity for teachers not only to win the trust of their students, but also to use that very trust (honestly, of course) in bolstering the legitimate confidence of their students. Simple, quiet, exact words of encouragement judiciously given for craftsmanly excellence—these are worth a great deal to the young men who receive them, quite as much as public mention, ribbons, or gold medals.

All praise, indeed, should be given as objectively as possible. A teacher should never gush. Real men—and students rightly consider themselves such—abhor sentimentality of any sort, even the "hard-boiled" kind; they do not relish being praised effusively and directly. Hence, the teacher who wishes to avoid both the venial sin and the blunder of flattery while still acting charitably, must praise the student's accomplishment, not the student. And this praise should take the form of an accurate, terse, factual description, not unlike a citation for heroism; an account which shows one craftsman's exact appreciation of the work of another. The student thus praised will not be embarrassed; rather, he will be strengthened by this true estimate of his achievement.

The student should never, of course, be publicly humiliated; he should never be "bawled out" before others. A sarcastic open reprimand can do only one of two things: hurt and dishearten the good student, or anger and harden the poor. Even private correction should be charitable: the stupidity must be treated as no more dangerous than it is; nor must it be prejudged as malice. Every correction, being a shock, should be broken like other bad news, gently; it should be preceded by praise for whatever was good in the methods, intentions, or performance under consideration. Moreover, corrections should be tempered to the person concerned: heavy enough for the callous; light enough for the sensitive. In short, all punishments should be corrective and diplomatic.

If the morale of a student is raised by his being shown that he is worthy of some respect even in being punished, it is also raised when he is shown that he is a member of a glorious organization. And here the teacher can use the methods not only of the military leader, but also those of the Apostolic. As an officer does with a soldier, the teacher can make every student feel sure of his fellows; this, by showing him: that they are essentially like him, hence as reliable as he is; that they are like him in going through the same curriculum, performing the same kinds of tasks, receiving the same discipline, living as a community, all unified by the same Charity, by sharing in the same religious rites, by constituting, as a group, a cell in the Mystical Body; all willing, indeed, to die, through Christ, that this, His Mystical Body, may spread upon the earth. The teacher in a Catholic college can develop an esprit de corps that is truly from God; an esprit de corps animated not merely by confidence but by Hope.

One of the greatest sources of confidence (in addition
to those arising from the student's proper knowledge of
himself and from his felt kinship with his fellow-students
in the Mystical Body) is that which springs from a reli-
ance on teachers who show that they are men of intelligence, good will, and Charity. The student rejoices when
he can feel that his leaders both know what they are doing
and act with Christlike love, sharing, as well as they may,
in the Wisdom and the Love of the Holy Ghost.

Obviously, students will believe in and trust a superior
when they see that he knows what he is doing. Not that he
need be a great artist in his field; but he must be a great
artist *as a teacher* in that field. No football player feels
that his coach should play as well as he himself does; but
he does feel that his coach should have played the game
fairly well at one time and should be able to *coach* extremely well. Every teacher must show that he "has been
through the mill," that he knows as much about his art
as a good teacher should know; that he is one with his students through sympathetic experience. The more he can
draw them out and cause them to work "better than they
knew how," the more will he win their respect; and the
more will he inspire not only their trust in him but also
their confidence in themselves and in their whole training.
The good teacher must show that he knows three things:
how a thing is done; how to do it himself very well; and
how to coach others to do it exceptionally well. At the
moment when students are convinced that they are in the
hands of a master of such skill, at that moment are they
strengthened by a profound access of courage.

The teacher must also show that he is, in two senses

of the word, good-willed: that he is strong-willed; and that he is kindly—literally, a foster-father. He must show that his heart is as strong as his head: that he is a man of humility and Charity, hence a man of self-control and fortitude; that he does not get rattled easily; that he is decisive; that he has coolness and poise; that he can command and enforce legitimate discipline, not being a "softy." His students must feel that he is human, just, and kind; that he plays no favorites; that he does not spare himself; that he never exercises his authority for the sake of exercising it. Nor must he show signs of effort: his students should rejoice in seeing him exercise his powers easily and naturally, neither strutting nor posing, on the one hand, nor weakly going through the motions of being a teacher, on the other: students like neither the "grandstanders" nor the colorless.

Besides being master of his own art, the teacher should show by example what it is to be a sufficient master of all the other arts. *He must be something of a model, both as teacher and as man,* symbolizing the kind of person the student should be after graduation. If the student is an apprentice in the art of living a fully Catholic life, the teacher should be enough of a master of that art to make it clear and appreciable. He must show in his life that the aims of the college are both attainable and very much worth while, so that students will remain confident that they are being trained for the right purpose by the right men.

Teachers must therefore inspire confidence in themselves, not merely as teachers but also as persons. They must show by manner, posture, gesture, speech and apparel that they know "what it is all about" and that they are "regular." There are two reasons for this: the first is that men believe the evidence of the senses and react to it automatically; the second, that a leader himself maintains his own confidence by acting as if he were what he is supposed to be.

Consider posture, for instance. The teacher who maintains a lackadaisical or limp or stiff or awkward posture thereby prompts the men under him to infer that he is the kind of person his posture suggests: lazy or pusillanimous or harsh or inept. Furthermore because, as we have already noted, men in a nervous condition tend to imitate objective suggestions—suggestions from without—they will contract, like a disease, the posture of their leader. They will tend, first, to adopt his posture—limp, stiff, or whatever—and then to feel the emotions and desires that go with such a posture: laziness, the love of luxury, and so on. For it is a law of psychology that ideas, emotions, and actions (or physical postures) are all closely connected. The thought of hurrying, for example, causes one (a) to want to hurry and (b) to start making flustered movements. Similarly, the mood of hurrying causes one to think of reasons for hurrying and to start hurrying. Finally, merely moving hurriedly causes one to feel hurried and to think of the need for hurry. Each of these factors—thought, feeling, and action—is closely connected with the other two. The teacher, therefore, whose posture suggests the idea of weakness, stupidity, or coldheartedness also causes his men to think and feel weakly, stupidly, or self-centeredly, since he makes them adopt subconsciously the physical attitude which induces these kinds of thinking and feeling.

All of which implies that since a teacher wishes his students to trust him he must adopt a posture that is worthy of that trust and that also *infects* them with it. His posture must therefore be easy, natural, and erect, signifying that his mind is at ease, well-poised, aggressive. He should maintain neither the jelly-fish nor the ramrod back, but a natural posture of intelligent, graceful, athletic alertness —head high, eyes level: an attitude of unselfconscious leadership. The fear that he may thereby induce his men to adopt, imitatively, an attitude of arrogance is not one to take seriously, for the reason that every student has to command at all times at least one person: himself.

What is true of posture is also true of facial expression, gesture, voice, and the rest: these must imply that the teacher is skilled and confident; and they must induce the students to adopt the right attitudes for skilful and confident work.

The ideal teacher is thus a good actor, especially a good pantomimist. He avoids every expression or gesture that might indicate that he is not at all times master of himself —that he might lose his head either through bewilderment or anger. All students realize that a stiff person who moves fixedly or slowly is likely to be a one-track mind, probably self-centered, unaware of others, inflexible, easy to bowl over. On the other hand, the teacher who moves too fast, who gestures excitedly, who starts to do one thing and then does another, who fumbles, taps, or drums with his fingers, who keeps looking at his watch, rubbing his eyes, playing with his glasses, and so on—this teacher betrays the fact that he lacks poise, the dignity of his rank, self-control, the ability to concentrate, a sense of order, and even natural courage. If the slow, angular teacher infects his students with a slow, angular awkward-ness and oxlike inflexibility, the excitable, bird-like teacher infects his students with the jitters and with the subcon-cious bewilderment and apprehension that go with them. Ideally, then, a teacher's action should be deliberate, de-cisive, natural, and smooth—graceful, business-like, and absolutely unaffected. Gestures, like words, should be few, direct, neat, effortless, and appropriate. Like all other externals, they should be easy-going enough to suggest that the teacher is a human and reasonably humorous person—neither a mere machine with no heart nor a fuddy-duddy who is so worried by his responsibility that he can never take time out for a laugh.

The voice should also meet the requirements laid down for gesture and expression. It should be deliberately pitched lower than usual, for several reasons. First of all, students naturally associate a deep, low voice with man-liness. Such a voice suggests that the speaker's vocal or-gans are at ease, relaxed; hence that he is, himself. For just as a shrill voice suggests fright (which does, in fact, cause the vocal organs to contract and emit shrieks) so a low voice suggests self-confidence (which causes the vocal organs to relax and send forth deep, easy tones—"in full-throated ease"). Whereas the high voice makes a listener subconsciously tighten his own throat and hence feel the fear and think the apprehensive thoughts that go with such a contraction, the low voice does just the opposite: it takes the tension out of his throat and sets him to feeling at ease and thinking confidently. Again, as with gestures, the voice should be neither hurried nor slow; neither weak nor harsh: it should neither stammer nor drag; neither bark nor fade. Rather, it should be clear, easy, natural, decisive, unaffected, warm. In brief, it must be both authoritative and fatherly.

The teacher need not be a great orator—in the usual sense of that term; in fact, he might better not be. For when faced with something to be done, men feel about their leader somewhat as Orville Wright felt about the parrot when he said that of all the birds it was the best speaker and the poorest flier. The teacher should speak and write simply and forcefully—showing that he is a man not of words but of action. His eloquence should result mainly from his full appreciation of the ideals he is imbuing, from his love of his art, from his knowledge and love of his students, and from his Charity. The highest motives, those of love, can be appealed to strongly without recourse to flowery rhetoric or bombast. What is good enough for Homer and the biblical writers is good enough for the teacher: his style should be as direct and racy as his ideas are heroic and profound.

Above all, the teacher must show that he has a full appreciation not only of his position (which the Fathers put second only to the priesthood) but also of the whole process in which he is engaged. He must see that his work is that of a spiritual foster-father concerned with restoring his student-sons, in Christ, to the integrity lost at the Fall and training them, despite their weakness and any "disgrace with fortune and men's eyes," to share in the work of the Trinity. With the Fall, man lost the Wisdom that can only be gained again through Faith; hence the teacher's task is to teach all things as ancillary to Faith. With the Fall, man became subject to infirmity and despair; hence the teacher's task is to enable him to regain, in all humility, the confidence of heroic action as this flows from

Hope. With the Fall, man lost his direct connection with God, as well as with Nature, through a loss of Charity; hence the teacher's task is to fill his mind and heart with that Charity, enabling him to live by it at all times.

And in thus nurturing the student, his foster-child, the teacher must think in terms of the peace, the love, and the joy of Nazareth. For, in a sense, the Catholic college is another Seat of Wisdom, and he is another St. Joseph in whose care has been put another Christ.

CHAPTER SEVEN

SUMMARY

THE GIST of this book can now be stated concisely in terms of the following summary outline:

In the first chapter it was suggested that a Catholic college should train for a Catholic way of life; that this way consisted of following a vocation, no matter what one's work, as a living member of the Mystical Body of Christ; and that, consequently, the Catholic college must be designed to train its students in the various arts, spiritual and secular, required by this way of life.

In the second chapter the material on which the Catholic college had to work was analyzed and found to be a young, good-hearted American boy, somewhat tainted by Philistinism.

In the third chapter a course of studies was suggested based primarily on the findings of the first two chapters; a curriculum in which the two main studies were applied theology and applied philosophy.

In the fourth and fifth chapters it was shown that all the courses of the curriculum could be integrated in two ways: primarily, in terms of Charity; secondarily and subordinately, in terms of skill.

In the sixth and seventh chapters it was suggested that the teacher must be regarded mainly as "coach, master, captain, and foster-father," with all the qualities which these characterizations imply.

The remaining chapters will be devoted to incidental suggestions and probable objections.

CHAPTER EIGHT

OBJECTIONS

THE COMMONEST OBJECTIONS to the plan here proposed are these: that it is not realistic enough; that it will get good results, but only a narrow range of results; that it would be difficult to put into effect; and that it slights the liberal arts. There is also, of course, the always to be expected objection that the plan is no good as a whole because it is faulty in this or that of its parts.

To deal with the last objection first: it is much like saying that the idea of an anthology is of no value simply because the anthologist forgot to include some author whom a great many readers like. Perhaps this whole plan of the Catholic college is fundamentally and radically wrong; if so, it is to be rejected for that reason. But it should not be rejected simply because this or that educator would prefer this or that subject, this or that method, to those suggested. For the author himself could object to it on that score; had he merely followed his feelings in the matter, he might have presented a somewhat different design: he would have liked very much to include in the curriculum (to give but one example) a course on Dante; but he put the suggestion aside as incongruous with the whole general plan of the college. He therefore asks the reader not to judge the plan as a whole merely in terms of some one part of it.

The objection that the program is not realistic enough seems, at first sight, to be very well raised; it would appear to be a more formidable objection than the first. The answer to it is that when we are faced with only two main alternatives in a situation and discover that we cannot take one, we see that the truly realistic thing to do is to take the other. If the big club chair looks comfortable but you have urgent business elsewhere, you are realistic if, instead of trying to doze in it for a few minutes, you go about your perhaps not very pleasant business. So here, in education: the post-war period is going to present us with only two choices: either to run away from a plague-spot for a comfortable doze or to find our happiness in cleaning it up. Are we to tell every student that we shall train him in the arts of getting ahead of the other man and dodging the dirty work? Are we to train him in the arts of scientific or aesthetic or scholarly escapism— showing him how, by conforming safely to an iniquitous system based on greed and injustice, he can be assured of some leisure for tasting the sweets of culture? Are we to tell him that he should feel free to take refuge in some metaphysical world of abstraction and romantic delight, after a day spent in grudging toil? Or are we to train him to find his happiness in humbly and skilfully playing the Good Samaritan? Must not the college which turned out the Getter and Appreciator yield to the college which turns out the Giver and Server? Conditions being what any realist should be able to see they are, namely those of a global plague-spot, shall we be training our students for anything but tragedy if we do not get them to enjoy doing the nobly charitable thing in the satisfyingly right way, with no thought of immediate personal gain, no care for "success," no complacency in a "higher standard" of mere physical and mental comfort? What, after all, is as real-

istic as facing the facts and dealing with them properly—
even when that means dealing with them idealistically?

But, to raise the next objection, is not the training here
proposed too narrowing, too religious, to enable a student
to live as richly and fully as he will wish, as he should wish,
to live? Will he not be concentrating too closely on a few
values, thus losing many others?

It would, of course, be possible to answer these questions simply and conclusively with the words of Our Lord,
"Make it your first care to find the kingdom of God, and
his approval, and all these things shall be yours without the
asking"; but it is possible also to show, specifically, that the
young Catholic can be promised all the values which others
seek and certain higher ones which they do not even dare
seek. Every Catholic, if he will just be a full Catholic, can
expect to have life, and have it more abundantly even in
this life than would anyone else similarly circumstanced.

The naturalistic thinker says that he alone can truly
enjoy nature; yet who had a greater appreciation of nature
than St. Francis? The Epicurean says that he alone can
offer you the fullest pleasures of food and drink; yet who
has the greatest Feasts? and who makes the best wines?
who has filled the art museums of the world with works
of radiant loveliness? The great danger of the monastery
and of the guild system is, indeed, not that they fail in
material matters but that they succeed almost too well.
The Stoic points to his ancient heroes of state and his
modern heroes of science; but which of these can equal
St. Paul, Father Damien, and The Little Flower? The
humanist offers us his achievement of a measured life; but
what saintly life is not lovelier in the deep rhythms of its
self-abnegation and its Hope? What humanist would have

put the Canticle of Canticles in among his sacred works? The liberals offer what they call freedom; but what man is more free than he who is free from vice?

The well trained Catholic may look forward to enjoying all the beauties of the world, for he can see Beauty everywhere; all the best of man-made goods, for he can assure the disposition of heart and of mind best suited to producing things of the highest quality; all the joy of human love, for he knows how to love; delight in a well lived life, for he has an understanding of true norms of conduct; the contentment of true freedom, for he knows in what this consists, and the Truth has made him free.

But above and beyond all this, he may hope for more than all the -isms put together dare promise: the joy of being an adopted son of God, one with Christ in the Eucharist, Member of the Mystical Body, Sharer, even in his daily life, in the Work of the Blessed Trinity. All hungers, instincts, drives, tendencies, all hopes, all Hope will be answered if he but believe and train himself, in Christ, to be fit for, if never deserving of, all these forms of satisfaction, delight, contentment, peace, and joy.

"And yet," comes the objection, "since the world does not recognize these truths, since it does not base its system of education on them, will not a boy who goes to your college be handicapped? Can your college give him a Bachelor of Arts degree that would be universally held acceptable? How will your graduates be able to fit into the scheme of things as they are now? Will a boy be able to go on easily to advanced study or into a reasonably good position in the business world from the Catholic college described here?"

The answer is that in a world not so much interested in Truth, Sanctity, and Charity as in Facts, Success, and Competition, a well trained Catholic graduate will naturally have a somewhat harder time than will a well trained agnostic. But even so, the lot of the boy who graduates from the kind of institution described in this book would be far better than might at first be supposed. Such a boy would not, to be sure, be able to enter directly most graduate or professional schools; but he might enter most liberal arts colleges as a Senior, certainly as a Junior. At the very least, he would have a full college education far better than that of most Bachelors of Arts, although he might have officially only a junior college diploma. If he goes into business, this will ordinarily be all that he needs, as the astonishing growth of the junior colleges in this country just before the war proves. If he goes out for an A. B. degree, he will get it at the same age at which most students get it, twenty-one; and he will get it with honors. If he goes in for advanced scholarship (the only kind that counts in the world of scholarship) he will certainly complete his work for a Doctorate a year or so ahead of most students, who ordinarily take five years, since he can use his Junior and Senior years in the liberal arts college to this end. It is, in fact, hard to see how the training here proposed would in any way hold a student back, especially in a world pretty much disgusted with the present educational system; rather, it should "give him the jump" on his fellows in both the professional and the business worlds.

As for the liberal arts: the question of what exactly is to be taught at a Catholic college would be easy to answer were it not for the tendency of some readers to judge proposals in terms not so much of what ought to be as of what they themselves are used to.

Let it be said at once, therefore, that the curriculum presented here was not designed either to please or displease the defenders of the liberal arts (although, in truth, this curriculum would be far more liberal, in the best sense of the word, than are most curricula to which it has been lately applied). No; the present curriculum was designed with only one intention, that of providing the type of training required for fulfilling the purposes outlined in the first part of this book. It is not either in line with or against any -ism—progressivism, essentialism, traditionalism, vocationalism—being simply for the turning out of good Catholics.

It is not, moreover, a be-all or end-all. It is not based on the presumption that a student who has gone through any set of courses is finally educated. It is rather based on the assumption that one of the main marks of an educated man is that he knows he is always just beginning his education, whatever heights he reaches. If students, having "got through" at eighteen, feel (as well they might) that they need four years or so more of college—good; let them go on and master all the other arts, private or professional, that they may need or be able to afford. No Catholic college should even give the impression that an education can be "completed"—that any curriculum can be, in any real sense, final. It is quite possible, indeed, that the curriculum here described may seem, to some at least, not merely incomplete, but deficient; inadequate to the turning out of a young man of "broad and deep culture"; not humanistic enough to be truly liberal; but, after all, that is not its purpose. Its purpose is to turn out a skilful and charitable Christian.

Even so, the education here described does seem, on close inspection, quite as liberal as any now being given— if we understand the word *liberal* in the sense in which it was first and most often used in the past. Aristotle, who is one of the first to use this term, tells us, in Book I of his *Metaphysics,* that the liberal arts first flourished in Egypt, because the priestly class there were liberal, that is, "free" men in the sense of being free from economic worries. Certain arts they saw to be necessary for every civilized man to master: the arts of reading, writing, speaking, measuring, finding the time, philosophizing, trying to foretell the future, conducting religious ceremonies, and so on. Hence the principles governing these arts they felt should be searched for deeply. But men who are worried about the necessity to get something done immediately, so as to satisfy some pressing need, have not the leisure (let it be recalled again that the Greek word from which we derive our word *school* means leisure) in which to investigate these principles thoroughly. Those men alone who can work in peace, quietly, with little or no thought of immediate results, can be free enough to investigate ultimate principles and pass them on to whatever other men are free enough to master them: the liberal arts are the arts prosecuted, formulated, and taught by men economically free to other men who are economically free.

Obviously, then, a liberal education is one which results when it is possible for a teacher to say to a student: "Forget time. We have all the time in the world. You do not have to worry about acquiring the kind of information which will enable you to get a good job shortly after graduation. Nor do I have to spend most of my time getting a higher degree or investigating or writing books, while teaching you, as it were, on my off days. My finances are also well enough taken care of to assure me the necessary leisure for full-time teaching. And your parents, of course, do not want you to be taking purely utilitarian subjects; they are anxious to have you mature at your own normal pace and develop those skills required for wise living, even if they do not help you to become a go-getter." But education can hardly be liberal, in any proper sense of the term, when the teacher must say to the student: "All right, my boy, just remember: we haven't much time. We have only four years in which to 'cover the ground.' In the course of that time, you must cram as much generally useful knowledge into your head as possible: information that will make you an all round success in the social as well as the business world. Take advantage of your opportunity here, and memorize as much as you can. Don't waste too much time on any one subject, or on mastering any one point in a subject: you have to cover the ground as a whole, get your credits, and try to get at least a *cum laude* degree. Meanwhile, you should make the kinds of contacts that will prove useful to you in after life. I can't spend much time with you outside class; I have my degrees to get, my books to write, my government advisory jobs to fill, my family to support as best I can. Please keep in mind that your parents are spending a great deal of money on you, and they expect results."

Perhaps the course of training set forth in this book is not to be found in most liberal arts colleges at present; but perhaps, too, it is liberal in that it frees students from mental, moral, and spiritual servitude. However it is to be characterized, may it have the good fortune to be judged on its own merits; may it be judged in relation to what it sets out to accomplish rather than in relation to what it does not.

MISCELLANY

ALTHOUGH IT WOULD BE POSSIBLE to go exhaustively into minor questions concerning such things as the selection of the members of the faculty, marking, degrees, entrance requirements, endowments, extra-curricular activities, ceremonies, and equipment, the result might well be to distract the reader from the main points of the plan here presented. Hence, in this appendix these questions, though raised, will be left for the reader to decide for himself.

Faculty. Questions which seem to occur to many people here are these: Should not the faculty be predominantly lay, for are not students doubly edified when they find that Catholicism is just as large a determinant of the life of a layman as it is, though in a different way, a determinant of the life of a priest? Should not priests be freed from teaching secular subjects (including the higher branches of philosophy) so that they may live more fully the life to which they are dedicated? Is it possible to do justice to two professions at once: to the law and to teaching? to medicine and to teaching? to the priesthood and to teaching? Is there a real dearth of good Catholic lay teachers—or are they frequently driven to teaching in non-Catholic institutions because there are no other positions open to them? Are they very prone to lapse into heresy, even in the teaching of theology? Should not the clergy be mainly busied with the conducting of normal schools for lay teachers, training these especially in the theology required for the proper teaching of every subject in a Catholic manner?

Endowment. The writer believes that the maximum endowment needed for establishing, from the ground up, an ideal Catholic college—one with no more than two hundred students—would be about $1,700,000; whereas, the minimum endowment would be about $50,000; this latter for an experimental college to be set up inside an already existing institution.

Tuition. Fantastic as this may sound, there should be no immediate or compulsory tuition fees. Students who could pay immediately would naturally be expected to do so; otherwise, students would be merely asked (never "dunned") to pay for their tuition some time within ten or so years after graduation. For no college career should be overshadowed by financial considerations. And that Catholic institution rightly deserves to fall, the graduates of which feel so little gratitude for its training, and have so little Charity, that they do not even keep it in being.

Extra-Curricular Activities. Should not students be required to do as much of the running of their whole community as possible, training themselves thereby in the economic, political, social, and ethical management of any institution—putting into immediate practice the theories they learn in their courses?

Ceremonies. Many questions could be raised about these; exactly how could they be scheduled so that students could live the life of the Church daily, and so on; but perhaps the following should suffice: Should not every student be required to take an oath of Charity, in public with his fellows, on entering college, and then, at graduation, another, on entering the world—both of them to be like the oath taken by soldiers and doctors, except, of course, that they would be phrased in terms of Charity, the Mystical Body, Christ the King, and the Trinity?

Equipment and Buildings. Here we face the questions: What should the student's college be to him; hence, what should it look like in order to be that fully? The answer, in the writer's opinion, is that it should be enough of an industry to enable the student to learn, at first hand, the meaning of hard work and business management; enough of a self-governing city to enable him to learn in it the rudiments of politics; enough of a laboratory to enable him to learn scientific method; enough of a museum, a theatre, and a concert hall to enable him to learn how to appreciate the fine arts; enough of a guild workshop to enable him to learn the fundamentals of professional craftsmanship and ethical cooperation; enough of a school to enable him to study and meditate; enough of a monastery to enable him to contemplate and praise God; enough of a refuge to enable him to relieve the needy, give alms; enough of a church to fill his needs as a Member of the Mystical Body. Its buildings, its rooms, should seem at all times what they are: parts of a great Christian home.

THE SOCRATIC METHOD

THE FOLLOWING so-called Thought-Provokers have been included so as to give the reader some idea of what is meant by the kind of Socratic Method which should be used in a Catholic college. The author has worked out, and used, other such questionnaires (for various other subjects); hence he feels sure that this method is one that can be followed universally. The samples offered in this chapter are to be considered merely as suggestive; the reader is asked to go through them so as to visualize, or gain an experience of, though not to judge finally, the general method they imply.

This method runs somewhat as follows: The instructor begins by reading the first case, or concrete example. Then he asks several members of the class the questions raised at the end of this case, questions which force the students to take some kind of stand—commit themselves to some principle or precept. Thereupon, the instructor, without commenting on the answers given, which are frequently in conflict, reads the next case and asks for the principle involved in it. The cases being chosen so as to make the students give, if possible, answers which seem contradictory, the class is soon faced with the necessity of adopting a compromise position, or of thinking out a vital distinction. Then, as each new case is read and commented on, the members of the class gradually work out a position which they all agree is sound; at the very least, they think out, face afresh, all the issues involved and most of the alternative answers, whether they arrive at final conclusions or not. In the end, they are ready to have the instructor take over and clarify the position that is best. The method is, in short, one of first-hand experience in the dialectics of discovery.

A Thought-Provoker on Private Property

Eleven men are shipwrecked. Nine save themselves in a life-boat. The tenth is about to drown when he finds one of the timbers from the wreck. As he is rejoicing in his good fortune, the eleventh man swims up. The piece of wood will not support two men. The eleventh takes it away from the tenth. Has he a right to do so? If so, why? If not, why not?

Ten of the men land on an island. The island is found to be inhabited by monkeys. They were there first. Do they therefore own the island, or do the men?

The men apportion the island equally. Then, a few years later, ten more shipwrecked men land on it. Have these any right to claim ownership in it? Suppose they say that the first ten men have no more right to the island, except for the improvements made on it, than had the monkeys. Would they be right? If the second group overpowered the first group when the first group suggested that the second become slaves, would the action be just?

Some years later, two thousand people are shipwrecked on the island, it being capable of supporting only two hundred. Who now owns the island? Suppose the two thousand are small children. Does that fact make any difference?

Is there any likeness between these conditions and a depression? How, if at all, do the two conditions differ?

Suppose that a man and his wife are sent by a rocket to a new planet. Do they own that planet, animals and all? Is everything theirs? If they have children, do those children acquire right to property only because the parents give it to them? And, similarly, do the grandchildren acquire property, own things, simply because it has been given to them by their parents? If they all agreed that the property belonged to everyone, but that each person would be allowed to use whatever he came upon first and managed without harm to others—would that be a state of private property?

In what, then, does the right of private property consist?—In having got there first?

A Thought-Provoker on Government Interference

A man strikes oil on his property. Oil is desperately needed. He refuses to sell until his price, which is high, is met. Is he justified in this? Can he set his own price?

A man has the capital wherewith to run a factory in a small town. His employees depend entirely on the salaries which he pays them. Nor have they been trained for other than his kind of factory. He threatens to invest his money elsewhere unless he can set the salaries and the conditions under which these men work. Has he the right to do this?

A man has unique skill or strength. He also has the capital which would enable him to get along without working. Others—sick and weak—need his help. Has he the right to set all the conditions of payment and work?

Have groups of oil-owners, capitalists, professional men, or laborers the right to organize and lobby so as to make sure that they can get their own prices and conditions?

One candidate for the office of representative uses as his main argument the promise that he will win the greatest possible privileges for his constituents. His opponent counters with the promise that he will simply prevent other groups than his own from getting special privileges. Which would you vote for? Which man *ought* you to vote for?

What is the government for:

    (a) to grant special favors to this or that group?
    (b) to assure complete freedom to all groups, letting them fight for supremacy and determine their own prices, regardless of the needs of others?
    (c) to prevent any group or groups from harming the others?
    (d) to strike a compromise between these three functions?

What is government interference?

A Thought-Provoker on Efficient Causality

You are watching a game of billiards, and you notice that when the cue-ball hits the object-ball, the cue-ball slows down—sometimes even stops. Would you say that when the cue-ball did stop, it had more successfully transferred its motion to the object-ball than when it did not stop?

A friend pulls out a cigarette and asks for a light. You strike a match and hold it to the end of his cigarette, so that this begins to burn. Would you say that the flame had been transferred from the match to the cigarette? Is the flame of the match diminished by exactly the same amount as the flame of the cigarette?

You wish mental stimulation; so you leave the billiard-room and go into the library, where you pick up a copy of *Don Quixote* and read it. Having finished a couple of chapters, you find yourself refreshed. Has the book, or Cervantes, lost energy by this process, an energy which you gained?

You are anxious to celebrate the end of a great war. On receiving news of victory, you and your friends go to a place where you have piled up the materials for a great bon-fire. You apply the match to the fuse which, in turn, sets off the pile. Is the flame that then burst forth simply the amount of flame that was drawn off from the match?

If you take all the heat out of water, you will have, of course, ice. Then, if you bring your hand near to this substance, your hand will feel a positive chill. But physics tells us that cold is nothing but the absence of heat. How can the absence of an energy transfer itself to the senses; how can a non-existent thing make the senses respond to it positively?

In cutting bread, you lose control of the knife and cut your finger. You feel a pang of pain. Was the pain on the edge of the knife, so that when the knife touched the pain nerve, the pain was somehow transferred from the knife edge to the mind?

If a teacher does not transfer his knowledge, or convey it, what does he do?

A Thought-Provoker on Government Control

During the war, you, who are a skilled master of wrought-iron work, find that priorities restrict, first, your material, giving you not enough metal with which to fill your orders. Has the state a right to do this?

After a while, the state takes over your factory, using it to make gun-fittings. Has the state a right to do this?

Then you are inducted into the army and sent back as a member of the engineering corps to supervise the making of the fittings. Has the state a right to do this?

Finally, you are told by military men just what fittings to make and just what methods to use in making them—being given standard blue-prints, routing schedules, job-analyses, and so on. Is this unjust?

As a result of all this, you now no longer are a full artist: the selection of materials, designs, methods, and purposes has been taken out of your hands. But by all this voluntary cooperation (patriotically inspired) you and others like you have been able to turn out vast quantities of armament which enable your soldiers to win the war. Now, after the war is over, the State comes to you and says: "Stay in uniform, but this time in civil uniform, and help us win the permanent *economic* war—the war against poverty, slums, and so on. We shall continue, of course, to choose the materials, methods, designs, and purposes for you." What would be your answer? Does even the Soviet Army in war time remain entirely under the management of the government? Can any one group of men act as both complete servants of the people and complete masters of them? both patrons and artist-designers, making all other men "hands"? Have we here an inkling of the real defense of private property—the necessity for its perfect handling and its perfect, its most artistic and meritorious, use?

What, then, are the limits of governmental confiscation of materials, indoctrination for intentions, control of methods, control of professions; and why are these the limits?